the
MOUNTAIN
in the
DESERT

Discovering God's Heart in the Wilderness of **Delay**

BOOK 1 OF THE **HEARTWORK SERIES**

the MOUNTAIN in the DESERT

Discovering God's Heart in the Wilderness of **Delay**

MIKE AND KELSEY DOMENY

*To our faithful Savior, Jesus Christ. All we need is you.
May You make much of Yourself through this book.*

*To you, who dare to follow Jesus, even when it leads to places you don't
want to go.*

Contents

A Note from the Authors

While this book is presented as the first book of the Heartwork Series, we understand different readers will find themselves in different phases of God's work in their lives. If you feel stuck in a "wilderness" season, where God seems distant or cruel, this book is for you.

Thank you for reading.

Mike and Kelsey

Chapter One

The Desert

"So what do you do?"

It's a simple question that sends us into a panic.

One summer, I (Kelsey) found myself with a lot of time to chat with other guests during a wedding rehearsal for Mike's cousin, which Mike was officiating.

While the wedding party shuffled around, rehearsing the basic functions of walking, standing, and sitting, I passed the time with my sister-in-law and the girlfriend of one of the groomsmen. This beautiful young lady was a med student about to be placed in her residency program. I know this because her answer to "what do you do?" was simple and easy to remember. My sister-in-law was next, and I knew it was only a matter of time before the dreaded question reached my end of the bench.

I sighed and looked at the trees ahead of us, knowing my answer would land like a lead balloon. "A few years ago," I began, "God told us to rely fully on His provision. That meant no full time jobs. So, we spend our days following Jesus and seeking His kingdom believing that He will provide all we need."

The med student blinked. That wasn't an easily-digested small-talk answer. After a few false starts, she finally found the words, "Oh, that's nice." My sister-in-law bolstered my answer by assuring her we write books and speak.

I'm pretty sure the med student avoided conversation with me the rest of the day.

I get it. Living like this is not what anyone would plan. It certainly doesn't look like any plan I would come up with.

If it were up to me, back in 2020, when Mike released his first book, *Thrown Off Script: Turn Obstacles into Opportunities and Thrive in the Unexpected*, the world would have seen how relevant that book was during the pandemic; millions of people would have bought it and we would have shot overnight into international best seller status and become sought-after speakers. We would be on our fourth book deal by now and speaking to sold out rooms at two hundred events per year.

But alas, it was not up to me. Instead, we walked in circles of hopelessness, lack of purpose, drought of resources, loss of connections, and fatigue—mentally, physically, spiritually. Our future has felt indefinitely delayed. In the wait, we've cried out "Why, God, did you lead us here? This doesn't feel like where we're supposed to be. Honestly, we wish we could go back to where we came from."

That's our desert. What's yours? Do you feel like you've lost a sense of purpose? Maybe you haven't actually found it yet, and you've been wandering for a while trying to figure out where you fit in the grand scheme of life. Maybe you feel like God has let you down. Perhaps there was a time in the past when your future looked clear and certain, but circumstances have shifted and you now find yourself adrift, a little aimless, yearning to feel settled. And likelihood is, you're tired.

One thing we've noticed talking to people living in "desert seasons" is that if you're in one, you know it. You may not be able to profoundly describe it, but you know you're there. We're with you.

This book is not born out of acclaim and success. It's not full of reflections from the finish line. This book was written in the desert. The desert has driven us to God's Word, as we'll explain, and this is a compilation of what we've learned along the way. We know we don't have every answer you need. We're here to share with you in the struggle and point you, not to some proven path we've carved out to escape hard times, but to the heart of God who is beside you, behind you, and before you through it all.

In the chapters ahead, we'll follow the journey of God's people out of slavery in Egypt into the wilderness. For the Israelites, the desert was unbearably difficult, tedious, and painfully relatable. But in this desert was a mountain. In your desert wanderings, you, too, will encounter a mountain—a waypoint to stop and interact with God.

How can you make the most of the mountain in the desert? Let's learn from the man who knew deserts and mountains better than anyone. Moses.

Before Moses was, you know, *Moses*—the staff-wielding, sea-splitting, plague-bringing Moses, he was the angsty, adopted son of an Egyptian princess. Adopted, because he was actually an Israelite whose mother gave him up in an attempt to save him from a murderous Pharaoh. Angsty, because his fellow Israelites had been bitterly oppressed by the Egyptians for generations. For hundreds of years no prophets came bearing hope. No miracles indicated God was at work. Only long years of feeling forgotten.

For generations, the oppressed nation of Israel struggled with questions that still circulate today:

Is God even real?

Is God with us here or not?

Is God good?

These are painful questions to have to ask. No answers came. Only more suffering.

One day, Moses saw an Egyptian beating an Israelite. Rage surged. We can imagine a million thoughts racing through Moses' brain. *This isn't the way it's supposed to be! This isn't right! Why is God letting this happen? If He's not going to do something about it, I will!* He looked around. No witnesses. One strike. The Egyptian collapsed, blood soaking the sand.

Moses had the heart, but not the timing. He had the passion, but not the method. The king exiled him. His own people rejected him. "Who made you ruler and judge over us?" they cried.

When God seems absent, we get desperate. We act. We push. We try to force justice, healing, and change, because waiting while things fall apart feels unbearable. And if God won't move, we will. Even if it's messy. Even if it's wrong. Because doing something feels better than doing nothing.

Be still

This is a story of being still. It's about those times in our life when we can't go back to what *was*, but we aren't yet where we long to be. It's being delayed in the wilderness, living somewhere between Egypt and the Promised Land, stuck in the desert of "no longer, but not yet." Our hearts cry, "God, where are you?" and we start asking:

Is God even real?

Is God with me here or not?

Is God good?

People have been asking these questions for thousands of years. Throughout the Bible, God has answered these questions, but not always in the ways we expect or hope. His answer is to help His people discover His heart by bringing them through their literal and figurative deserts to stop and know Him. Or, in His words, "be still and know that I am God" (Psalm 46:10).

In the chapters that follow, we'll track the Israelites' journey through the desert and highlight the moments where God reveals who He is. As a result, we hope you will discover timeless truths that comfort and challenge you to recognize God's heart in your own desert seasons, camped in the shadow of God's mountain.

Chapter Two

The Sandals

Forty years. Moses had officially spent more time as his father-in-law's shepherd than as a son of an Egyptian princess. And he had nothing to show for any of it. His royal training and connections were cut off, and he didn't even own a single sheep he tended. Forty years into this lease of fleece was not an anniversary worth celebrating.

This wasn't Moses' dream job, but he was equipped, and did it well. A sheep fell in a crag in the rocks? No problem, Moses gripped his staff as leverage to get the sheep out. A lamb wandered off from the flock? Easy. Moses scampered his sandaled feet to secure the youngling and bring it back. A mountain lion encroached, craving a mutton dinner? He stood his ground and wielded his staff to fend off the beast.

Then one day, there was this bush. It was on fire, but not being consumed—a bewildering anomaly—and Moses couldn't resist an inspection.

"When the Lord saw Moses coming to take a closer look, God called to him from the middle of the bush, 'Moses! Moses!'" (Ex. 3:4).

When we get mail addressed to "Mr. Kelsey Domeny," or "Current Resident" we throw it away immediately because whoever sent it clearly does not know us. But when "Michael and Kelsey Domeny" are written on an envelope in Grammie Linda's handwriting, we're eager to open it because someone who knows us by name has taken the time to send us a message.

The Almighty initiated this life-changing conversation with Moses' name. God knew Moses' name. We're too quick to move on from this truth. "Yeah, guys. He's God. Of course He knows everything." But we invite you to stop and sit with this for a moment. The God of the universe knows *your* name.

God knows your name.

God knows your name.

No, that's not a printing error; it's repeated on purpose because it's worth reading again.

God. Knows. Your. Name.

Isaiah 43:1 ensures us, "Do not be afraid, for I have ransomed you. I have called you by name; you are mine." God knows your name and called you.

GOD DIDN'T START WITH A TO-DO LIST. HE STARTED WITH A RELATIONSHIP.

At this moment in time, while you read this, you may not be at a burning bush, but God is calling your name. He is inviting you to know Him as He already knows you. God is initiating a conversation. What will you do? How will you respond? What will be your answer?

When God had a mission for Moses, He didn't start with a to-do list. He started with a relationship.

Moses answered, "Here I am."

God replied with an odd directive.

"Remove your sandals for the place you are standing is holy ground" (Ex. 3:5).

This is the first time God spoke to His people in 400 years, and His first mandate was "take off your shoes." It seems weird, right?

"Can we get a bunny?"

I (Mike) blinked. Not only because Kelsey's question surprised me, but mostly because it was 10pm and I had just barely fallen asleep. Kelsey, apparently, had not.

"Because," she continued regardless of my blank face, "there's someone local who is looking to re-home their bunny." She was now expecting my verbal response.

"Uh... maybe? Can we maybe talk about it in the morning?"

"Okay!" Kelsey resumed typing on her phone with renewed fervor.

I half-expected to wake up to a bunny. Frankly, that would have been less overwhelming than what I actually woke up to: Kelsey's smiling face and four hours' worth of messages and research.

"His name is Rocket, and he's six months old. He's a male Holland lop, which everyone says is the nicest kind of rabbit. He comes with a hutch. And he's litter trained!"

Long story short, we have a bunny. And his name is now Cinnabun.

Cinnabun is the softest thing I've ever pet. The only improvement my family wishes upon him is that he would stay in one place long enough for us to pet him. He will respond favorably to treats; if I'm lucky, he'll jump into my lap for a couple seconds to eat a pumpkin seed there. But he has no interest in staying and socializing. As soon as the treat is done, so is the moment.

The bunny has no idea how much joy he would bring us—and himself—if he would stop and stay a while. Be loved. But no, he apparently has a thousand places to be, things to do, and predators to hide from in the living room.

When he jumps away, I can't help but sigh and wonder if that's how God thinks of me. If only I knew how much joy I would bring Him—and myself—if I approached Him and stayed a while. But no, I apparently have projects to complete, deadlines to meet, and screens to watch in the living room.

God wanted Moses to stay a while. Moses did remove his sandals. He stopped working. He shifted his focus. He relinquished the power to run off if one of the sheep needed rescuing. By taking off his sandals, he was giving his whole attention to God. God commanded Moses to remove his sandals so Moses would stop what he was doing, submit, and humble himself to God's will.

Sometimes God invites us to deserts because we're too focused on things outside of Him. When He tells us to stop, it's an invitation to "take off your shoes and stay a while." He wants to be with us, and He wants us to be with Him without distractions. We have to be still with Him to get to know Him. Especially when we aren't sure whether He's there or not.

When the people of Israel were convinced God had forgotten them, He went to Moses and said, "Look! The cry of the people of Israel has reached me, and I have seen how harshly the Egyptians abuse them. Now go, for I am sending you to Pharaoh. You must lead my people Israel out of Egypt" (Ex. 3:9-10).

Forty years prior, if God had gone to Moses and said, "Lead my people out of Egypt," Moses would have been *all for it*. How do we know? In the book of Acts, Stephen's speech before his martyrdom gives insight into Moses' motivation as a younger man.

Moses was taught all the wisdom of the Egyptians, and *he was powerful in both speech and action.* One day when Moses was forty years old, he decided to visit his relatives, the people of Israel. He saw an Egyptian mistreating an Israelite. So Moses came to the man's defense and avenged him, killing the Egyptian. *Moses assumed his fellow Israelites would realize that God had sent him to rescue them,* but they didn't. (Acts 7:22-25, emphasis mine)

Moses had put all the pieces together as a young man. He saw the plans of God at work.

He was an Israelite.

God miraculously preserved his life as a baby.

He lived in Pharaoh's house.

He had all the respect of those in power.

He had all the training he needed to be a leader.

Certainly, God had positioned him to rescue Israel! If God had appeared in a burning bush while young Moses was out on his daily chariot ride around the kingdom, Moses would have jumped at the chance to be God's man on the ground. He was ready and eager. He was trained and powerful. He was a man of action.

But God didn't speak to Moses when Moses was forty. When Moses was forty, God was silent. So Moses made himself the hero of his story and took matters into his own hands. He went from prince to outcast murderer in one hasty attempt to bring about God's justice.

Forty years *later*, God appeared and called Moses to the mission. But it had been so long since Moses had spoken before kings he had forgotten who he was. God was too late. In fact, the very things he once thought qualified him (powerful in speech and action) he now declared as reasons he was unfit to lead.

> But Moses pleaded with the Lord, "O Lord, I'm not very good with words. I never have been, and I'm not now, even though you have spoken to me. I get tongue-tied, and my words get tangled" (Ex. 4:10).

In his dejection, he rewrote his story and changed how he defined himself. Moses protested to God, "Who am I to appear before Pharaoh? Who am I to lead the people of Israel out of Egypt?" (Ex. 3:11)

When faced with God's calling for his life, Moses's first thought was his inadequacy. His initial response was self-doubt. His first question was, "who am I to do this thing?"

If I was in Moses' place, I would hope God would respond with, "Oh, don't be so hard on yourself! You're more capable than you think you are!" But God didn't explain why Moses was the right choice. God didn't try to build up his self esteem. He didn't even answer the question. Instead, God simply responded, "I will be with you" (Ex. 3:12). Moses was focused on who *he* was, what *he* had to offer, how it would work for *him* to carry out this plan. God was telling Moses to stop focusing on Moses. Instead, focus on the God who is with you!

My friend, God will be with *you*!

Is that encouraging? If so, wonderful. Rest in that. But we have to be honest, "God is with you" hasn't always felt like an exciting or comforting thought.

It reminds me of when a friend invited us to a fundraising dinner and shared excitedly, "Brandon Heath will be there!" Maybe you're familiar with his music, and that thought would excite you. Or maybe you're like us and thought, "Cool! Oh wait, did he say 'Brandon Lake?' No? So who's Brandon Heath? Should I be excited?"

We didn't know the artist. Some of his songs did ring a bell when we heard them. "Oh! Yeah I've heard this one." But knowing he would be at the banquet didn't fill us with anticipation.

If hearing the simple truth that "God will be with you," doesn't fill you with hope and encouragement, maybe God is to you like Brandon Heath was to us. You know some of His work. Psalm 23 is a classic. You listened to John 3:16 back in the day. But you haven't followed Him lately, and you haven't followed His work in a long time. At this point, you just don't really know who He is or what to expect when He shows up.

I Am

That's where Moses was. Hearing "I will be with you" didn't immediately get Moses on board with the plan.

> But Moses protested, "If I go to the people of Israel and tell them, 'The God of your ancestors has sent me to you,' they will ask me, 'What is his name?' Then what should I tell them?" (Ex. 3:13).

Less formally, Moses is challenging, "Okay, you'll be with me, but who are you? And why should I be excited?" In order to trust that having God with us is enough to get us through whatever comes our way, we need to know who He is. Fortunately there is nothing God wants more than for us to know Him and be with Him. He was eager to answer Moses' protest and ours.

> God replied to Moses, *"I Am Who I Am.* Say this to the people of Israel: I Am has sent me to you." God also said to Moses, "Say this to the people of Israel: *Yahweh,* the God of your ancestors—the God of Abraham, the God of Isaac, and the God of Jacob—has sent me to you.
> This is my eternal name, my name to remember for all generations." (Ex. 3:14-15, emphasis added).

In Hebrew culture, someone's name and their identity were intertwined. The foundational truth of a person was communicated through their name. The name God revealed to His people is "I Am."

Imagine being the Hebrews hearing this. After 400 years of silence, God was coming to rescue them and the personal and intimate name He gives them is "I Am." With His name, He is declaring, "I never left! I Am. I always was. I always will be. I Am! You didn't see me, but I've been here. You didn't hear me, but I have been listening. I am present. I am here. I am for you. There is no other God before me. I am God. I Am."

His Name is *I Am.* He is never changing. Always present. He had no beginning; He has no end. *That* is what the Lord revealed to Moses from that burning bush. And *that* is who is with *you* in your desert of delay.

All the answers to the hard, honest questions we ask are in His name:

Is God even real?

... I Am.

Is God with us here or not?

...I Am.

Is God good?

...I Am!

It is fundamental to who He is, that He is with His created, beloved people. Just as Moses first heard this name when he stopped and removed his sandals in front of the burning bush, God will bring your busyness to a halt to give you an opportunity to know Him. In order for you to meet Yahweh, He will ask you to remove your sandals and stop to get to know Him.

Take these opportunities! His silence is not punishment. Your waiting is not for your torment. Remove your sandals and stay a while. The God of the universe wants to spend some time with you free of distractions, goals, and striving. Just be with Him.

Be still and know I Am

Being with you and being known by you was Jesus' entire reason for everything He did. Discover this heartbeat in Jesus' prayer before going to the cross:

> I am praying not only for these disciples but also for all who will ever believe in me through their message. I pray that they will all be one, just as you and I are one—as you are in me, Father, and I am in you. And may they be in us so that the world will believe you sent me.
>
> I have given them the glory you gave me, so they may

be one as we are one. I am in them and you are in me.
(John 17:20-23a)

Listen to the intimacy He desires with us. He prays for oneness with Him, for us to be as close to Him as He is with the Father. In the same way the Father is in the Son, one in purpose and power, Jesus wants to be with you and me. This is a mind-blowing reality!

Verse 26 punctuates the point, "I have revealed you to them, and I will continue to do so. Then your love for me will be in them, and I will be in them." Jesus was and *still is* constantly revealing the Father to us, helping us to know Him.

What God wanted for Moses at the burning bush, He wants for us now: to be with Him and to know Him personally.

And as Psalm 46:10 urges us to "be still and know that I am God," we can recognize that when God leads us to the desert, it is so we can know Him in the stillness the delay offers.

What could happen if we embrace the wilderness? If we rest in the pause? If we didn't rush the wait? What if we took the time in the stop to get to know *I Am*?

Like a bunny choosing to stay, rest and be pet by his loving owners, maybe we can take the delay in this desert as a time to enjoy the presence of God. Instead of running to find what's next, or tick off boxes on a to-do list, what if we took off our shoes and stayed a while?

As we walk through the rest of the Exodus story we will witness God's unrelenting pursuit of His people. However, at this point of the story, Moses doesn't know Him yet; their relationship is just starting. So if you're a little shaky on whether God is with you or if it makes a difference, you're in good company. If stopping to be still and just be with God feels uncomfortable and unfamiliar, it's okay. Stick with us; stick with Moses and the people of Israel. As God reveals His heart to His people, know He is the same yesterday, today, and forever (Hebrews 13:8). That means anything He revealed to the Hebrews, He is revealing to you, too.

While you walk through this desert season, however long it may last for you, our prayer is that you would seize the opportunity to be still and get to know God's heart. Recognize this desert as a place of relationship.

Chapter Three

The Staff

You can hear the self-doubt in Moses' voice, "What if they don't believe me or listen to me?"

God asked, "What's in your hand?"

"A shepherd's staff," Moses replied. We can almost hear the tone in Moses' voice. *What, this old thing? It's just a staff...it's nothing. It's a tool of shepherds. Nobodies. People like me.*

In the midst of his barefoot, knees on the ground, humbling and intimate time with God, Moses was still holding on to what he knew: his staff. And right in the middle of the encounter, God called him out.

"What's in your hand?"

"I am not qualified! You have the wrong people!" was a daily protest in my prayers.

God laid on our hearts a plan for a coaching community to help people say "yes" to what God put on their hearts. It was called The Grove. For three beautiful years, we led this small but mighty community of authors, artists, business owners, missionaries, and more. The stories of their faith, their struggles, their victories, and their pursuit of Jesus even when it didn't make sense, kept us going.

The Grove began with a business plan that was as clear as Noah's instructions for the ark. And, like Noah, God told us to build it and trust Him to fill it. The right people found us, fumbled and flourished in their own walks of faith, and we loved them every moment. Those who nestled in the shade of The Grove were challenged by God in profound, life-altering ways. And so were we.

But eventually, the ark came to rest, the flood was over, the structure was dismantled and the wood used for the next phase of civilization as Noah and his family rebuilt their lives. And, in the spring of 2025, as we prayed about The Grove and our future, we were devastated to admit our time with them was done. When God made it clear that we needed to stop coaching this community, I was heartbroken. I felt like a failure. I felt like I was giving up. It was the best thing we had ever done, and I wondered if it would be downhill from there. I didn't want to let it go. Letting go meant losing my identity, my purpose, my Kingdom work all over again. The pandemic had already stripped us of those things earlier; I couldn't believe another desert was our next destination.

But obedience brought us into it, and obedience demanded we leave it. It was so hard to walk away, but that dream needed to be released so we could move on to what God had planned next. There is a time to move into the ark and a time to move on from it.

What's in your hand?

As Moses stood in front of the Lord, barefoot and dumbfounded, he grasped his shepherd's staff as God issued a challenge. "Throw it down on the ground" (Ex. 4:3).

That's a loaded request. Throwing down the staff meant letting go, with no promise of getting it back. It wasn't about letting go of his successes and goals. This was the wilderness, after all. Any sense of pride from past accolades is long gone. No, the staff represented the past forty years of falling from favor: his ordinariness, his loss of status, and loss of purpose. The staff characterized the insecure stories in his head saying, "the best days are behind you; God has no use for you anymore."

Before moving on with the rest of the story, I think it's wise to ask, *What is my staff?*

Again, avoid cataloging your victories and wins, resources and experience, comforts and goals. Those need to be given to God, certainly, but I'm guessing your wilderness season is not characterized by such securities. No, your trusty tool as you've navigated your wilderness is likely your insecurity.

It says things like, "you're alone, things won't change, you're not enough, there's no future for you." Would it surprise you to hear that these deflating thoughts are just as prideful as ego-inflating ones? Pride means thinking of yourself contrary to what God thinks about you, and it's not limited to thinking too *highly* of yourself.

If we define ourselves as victims when God says we are more than conquerors (Romans 8:37), it's pride. If we dwell on our past failures when God says to forget the former things (Isaiah 43:18-19), it's pride. If we decide we are broken beyond repair when God says we are His masterpiece (Ephesians 2:10), it's pride. All of these attitudes reject our identity found in God's Word. And it's time to throw them down.

Throwing it down

Remember God's exact words when He looked at Moses' staff, the ordinary tool that represented the long years of ambiguity. He did *not* say, "throw it down," like we might say, "throw it away; you don't need it anymore." No, He said, "throw it down on the *ground*."

And do you remember what God said earlier about the ground? It's holy. God didn't discard everything from Moses' past. The forty years of shepherding were not for nothing. But it was time to throw them down on holy ground. It was time to release his past, and his plans, and his pride onto the place set apart for divine work.

An unexplainable miracle followed. A wooden staff became a snake. It turned into a snake that would later consume the work of the Egyptian magicians (Ex. 7:10-12). Quite literally, God's miraculous power would overtake and defeat the work of false gods. The incredible and awesome power of God would be on display through the humble shepherd's staff.

Moses' past wasn't being discarded. It was being renewed into something greater.

The three years we worked as coaches were not discarded. While we coached others, God was changing us into who we needed to be for the next steps ahead. When He told us to let that part of our lives go, it wasn't because we had failed as coaches; it was because it was time to do something greater with all we had learned in that season.

God is calling you to stop holding onto your past, your failures, your pain, your pride. He's preparing to use what you see as plain and unremarkable in your life to put His power on display through you.

When we submit all we are and everything we have to God, He takes ordinary things and does the extraordinary.

What happens next is almost more insane. God told Moses to grab the snake by the tail. Moses was a shepherd in the wilderness of Midian. We are confident this was not the first snake he encountered. Given the region, this snake was likely a cobra or a viper. Whatever it was, it was deadly and it was the size of a shepherd staff—easily six feet long! We know it was real, and we know it was scary, because Exodus 4:3 tells us, "Moses jumped back." He knew to keep clear of this thing!

Snake handling 101

We have not handled snakes, but we have watched Bear Grylls. He is a TV personality, famous for hosting "Man vs. Wild." He served in the British Army's Special Air Service, and was one of the youngest people ever to climb Mount Everest. He's a man who knows how to survive in a desert. When Bear Grylls encounters a snake, he never, ever grabs a snake by the tail. "Always pin the head," he would say. If you grab its tail, it can whip around and bite you in the face, and that's the last thing you'll see.

Moses had been navigating desert living for forty years. He probably knew how to handle snakes that slithered into the sheep pen. Pin the head. Make Bear Grylls proud. Yet God's instructions were clearly counter-intuitive: "Grab the snake by the tail."

Can you imagine? Moses stood there, facing the fire, no shoes on his feet, no staff to defend himself, a venomous snake on the ground. He was defenseless in a dangerous situation. Grab it by the tail? When God has stripped away what you usually depend on for safety and security, obeying His one scary command is the only thing left to do.

In these years of seeking the Kingdom first and not pursuing regular jobs, we haven't faced a literal viper, but we certainly have felt in danger. Our bank account has been down to $32 with rent due in a week. We've nervously anticipated months on end with no gigs, no plans, no predictable income. Amidst tear-soaked pillows in impossibly difficult situations as a result of following God, we've had two choices: 1) turn in fear and go our own way, or 2) keep doing what He says, even when it doesn't make sense.

In your desert, God will challenge you to throw down your staff. The results of your obedience may surprise or scare you. Did you obey because you thought obedience would get you out of your uncomfortable situation? Or did you obey simply because that's what God asked of you?

Now, the situation seems worse. "Not only am I stuck in the desert, but now there's a viper in front of me!" But God always provides a way out of the danger that results from your obedience. Don't be surprised, though, if His way out also requires scary obedience. Will you pick it up by the tail?

Moses did. Exodus 4:4 tells us, "So Moses reached out and grabbed it, and it turned back into a shepherd's staff in his hand."

IT IS CHANGED FOR GOOD. AND IT IS CHANGED FOR HIM.

But look at this. After this encounter, as Moses leaves the mountain, his staff is referred to as "the staff of God" (Ex. 4:20b). This is the beautiful fruit of this entire interaction! Moses' staff, representative of the past forty years of obscurity and desert-living, has been repurposed—the staff of God, for God's purposes—and Moses will continue to walk the desert in light of this transformation. *When God changes something, it is changed for good, and it is changed for Him.*

Be still and be changed

Remember, we encouraged you to consider your staff—the insecurities and past stories by which you've defined yourself. So who's responsible for transforming these things into the powerful "staff of God"? Is it up to you to throw them down and retrain your mind? Or is it up to God to do it in His time and His way? Which is it?

Paul, in his letter to the church in Ephesus, addresses this idea. "Since you have heard about Jesus and have learned the truth that comes from him, throw off your old sinful nature and your former way of life, which is corrupted by lust and deception" (Ephesians 4:21-23).

So there you have it! We have the responsibility to "throw off" the former way of life.

But Paul goes on to say in verse 24, "Instead, let the Spirit renew your thoughts and attitudes. Put on your new nature, created to be like God—truly righteous and holy."

God's Spirit is one One who does the work to renew your thoughts and attitudes, if you let Him.

So Paul's answer to "Which is it?" is an unhelpful "Yes." You have the responsibility of "throwing off" the old sinful nature and former way of life. Throw the staff on the ground. But remember, the ground is holy, so let the Holy Spirit do the renewing work only He can do. God is a master at upcycling old things and giving them new use. He can use any part of your previously lived story to complete His work in and through you.

But you can't leave it there. You have to, like Paul reminds us, "put on your new nature." That's scary. That's picking it up by the tail. Your new nature will have to yield to God's will from now on. Your new nature will have to submit to God's timing and plans, and give up credit and comfort, and flee from sin and temptation—some days better than others, but always striving for righteousness and unity with Jesus—until you're dead! That's not an easy commitment! But in exchange, you get to know the heart of God, I Am, as you walk as you are created to be—truly righteous and holy.

Chapter Four

The Lament

Moses set out on an unthinkable quest: return to the land in which he was an outlaw, confront a Pharaoh who had all the power, to free slaves who did not think God cared.

With the staff of God in hand, he arrived in Egypt and teamed up with his brother, Aaron. I bet Moses was more than a little excited to show the elders of Israel the signs God gave him. Sure enough, the staff turned into a snake and back again, and "the people of Israel were convinced that the Lord had sent Moses and Aaron. When they heard that the Lord was concerned about them and had seen their misery, they bowed down and worshiped" (Ex. 4:31). For the first time in 400 years, Israel had hope.

When you have felt like you're living under God's radar, it fills the heart with joy and worship to know that God sees you and is moving.

Of course, now that He sees me, He will help me, your heart rejoices.

My circumstances are about to change for the better!

I sought the Lord, and He heard, and He answered!

It's a wonderful thing when God sees you, hears you, and answers your prayers. The Israelites felt this as they listened to Moses. Worship and relief spread through the city as people recognized God had finally sent a prophet, a promise, and hope for freedom.

But the songs of praise were cut short when Moses approached Pharaoh.

God had warned Moses that He would harden Pharaoh's heart; but Moses could not have been prepared for what that would mean. Moses must have anticipated that God had prepared the way, and Pharaoh would agree easily to their request to let the Israelites go into the wilderness to worship Yahweh.

But Pharaoh mocked, "Who is this Yahweh? I don't know him." To make matters worse, he made matters worse. I can't tell the story any better than how it's written in Exodus. Pharaoh sent this order: "Do not supply any more straw for making bricks. Make the people get it themselves! But still require them to make the same number of bricks as before. Don't reduce the quota. They are lazy. That's why they are crying out, 'Let us go and offer sacrifices to our God.' Load them down with more work. Make them sweat! That will teach them to listen to lies!" (Ex. 5:7-9).

How did it unravel so quickly? God was moving! He sent a prophet! He confirmed His promise! Why did everything get *worse*?

Hope was met with humiliation and abuse. When God doesn't move the way we imagine, the disappointment can feel like a spiritual gut-punch—raw, confusing, and deeply personal.

After leaving my staff position at a megachurch, I (Kelsey) didn't trust church, and Mike and I both had a great deal of bitterness. The lead pastor exhibited narcissistic traits, and the treatment of staff was emotionally and spiritually abusive. The bitterness toward church was so strong it caused me to consider, for the first time in my life, *maybe I'm not a church person.*

That was 2021. It was a real "kick-you-while-you're-down" season after COVID-19 mostly shut down Mike's ministry and changed our lives completely.

It took everything we had to find another church, and the one we found was unmistakably where we were meant to be. Not to put too fine a point on it, but I heard an almost audible voice of God say, "you will worship here" as bitterness, unforgiveness, and heartsickness supernaturally melted off of me during a Sunday service. I had hope again, much like the Israelites when Moses first arrived in Egypt with news from God.

But if I knew what was really coming, I don't think I would have stayed.

Joining this new church led to one of our most difficult desert seasons.

After attending for a little more than a year, I was placed in leadership as the creative director. There were people on my team who hated me from the start. I was despised, lied about, gossiped over, and plotted against by other leaders in the church.

Physically, my body felt ravaged. I was sicker than I've ever been. I was exhausted. I gained stress-induced weight. I couldn't fall asleep, and when sleep did overtake me, I couldn't get up from my bed. This might sound like depression, but I had battled depression in my early twenties, and this was way worse. It was a force outside of myself. It was a spiritual attack on a level I never endured before. Mentally, I was on the brink of paranoia. Spiritually, I was heartsick. I didn't understand why God was allowing such darkness to attack me when all I wanted was to serve Jesus in His church.

My broken heart couldn't understand how God could let this continue. I wept into my pillow, night after night, *God, why did you send me here? God, why aren't you doing anything? Why are you letting this happen? Why is it getting worse?*

Moses cried out, "Why have you brought all this trouble on your own people, Lord? Why did you send me? Ever since I came to Pharaoh as your spokesman, he has been even more brutal to your people. And you have done nothing to rescue them!" (Ex. 5:22-23)

The hardest part of our dark church year was knowing beyond the shadow of a doubt that God had placed us there. We knew we were where God wanted us to be, but where He wanted us to be was painful—brutal, even. And it didn't feel like God was doing anything to rescue us.

Here's what God said to Moses, "Now you will see what I will do to Pharaoh. When he feels the force of my strong hand, he will let the people go. In fact, he will force them to leave his land!" And God said to Moses, "I am Yahweh—'the Lord.' I appeared to Abraham, to Isaac, and to Jacob as El-Shaddai—'God Almighty'—but I did not reveal my name, Yahweh, to them" (Ex. 6:1-3).

During the filming of the movie *The Princess Bride*, the director, Rob Reiner, instructed the cast to treat their characters as if they had a card behind their back the whole time. "Don't show the card, but let us know you have it by the way you look, respond, and treat the other characters." This produced a film full of characters who all had a glint in their eye—a look that said, "I know something you do not know."[1]

Here's a mysterious truth about God: He always has something behind His back He hasn't played yet. You never fully know what He's up to. He may not show you the card, but He will let you know He has it by the way He looks, responds, and treats you.

He even tells us as much! "My thoughts are nothing like your thoughts," says the Lord. "And my ways are far beyond anything you could imagine" (Isaiah 55:8).

God chose to keep His name, "I Am," a secret from even His close friend, Abraham. He didn't reveal this truth about Himself for hundreds of years. But now, the time was right. You can almost see a twinkle in God's eye as He plays his card.

Learn to recognize the glint in God's eye. In our desert seasons, we've found that God leaves noticeable traces of his attention throughout our journey. The way events transpire. The way a particular Bible passage shows up a few times in a week. The way our hearts lean in prayer. It's hard to describe, but there's a sense that God is up to something. We affectionately call it "God sauce." You can smell Him cooking.

Back in Egypt, things were looking bad for the Hebrews, but God's plan that was set in motion since Abraham remained unchanged. He knew something they did not know. Pharaoh was unknowingly setting the stage for God to show His power.

"I am the Lord. I will free you from your oppression and will rescue you from your slavery in Egypt. I will redeem you with a powerful arm and great acts of judgment. I will claim you as my own people, and I will be your God. Then you will know that I am the Lord your God who has freed you from your oppression in Egypt. I will bring you into the land I swore to give to Abraham, Isaac, and Jacob. I will give it to you as your very own possession. I am the Lord!" (Ex. 6:6-8)

Moses must have felt a breeze of encouragement and hope with this new revelation from God. He hurried to share this encouragement with his embattled people, "but they refused to listen anymore. They had become too discouraged by the brutality of their slavery" (Ex. 6:9).

IF YOU DON'T KNOW THE GOD OF THE WORD, THE WORD OF GOD IS HARD TO HEAR. The people who had dared to hope when Moses arrived on the scene now couldn't bear to hear more words from the Lord who had brought about greater depths of struggle. I can relate. God had led me, I followed, and I was so heartsick that I struggled to trust His words. *If you don't know the God of the Word, the Word of God is hard to hear.*

In the midst of the battle at church it took months before I (Kelsey) could read the Bible and draw any comfort. My heart was too heavy. When I did crack that binding, you can imagine how gut-wrenching it was when this passage left off the page:

> My suffering was good for
> me, for it taught me to pay
> attention to your decrees.
> (Psalm 119:71)

"My suffering was *good for me*"? I remember reading that and thinking before I could catch myself, "are you kidding me, God?" But then I read the full passage. I'm pasting it here. If you're like me, it can be easy to skip these long blocks of Scripture, but please do yourself a kindness and read this excerpt from God's heart straight to yours as you sit in your desert of delay. The single greatest thing I can pass on to you from my experience is how the Lord healed my heart. And that was through this very passage:

> You have done many good things for me, Lord,
> just as you promised.
> I believe in your commands;
> now teach me good judgment and knowledge.
> I used to wander off until you disciplined me;
> but now I closely follow your word.
> You are good and do only good;
> teach me your decrees.
> Arrogant people smear me with lies,
> but in truth I obey your commandments with all my heart.
> Their hearts are dull and stupid,
> but I delight in your instructions.
> My suffering was good for me,
> for it taught me to pay attention to your decrees.
> Your instructions are more valuable to me
> than millions in gold and silver.
> (Psalm 119:65-72)

This passage brought everything into focus. I wasn't the victim in my story after all: I was prideful, arrogant, and while God had given me an assignment to help the church, He was also working out the sin in my own heart. While arrogant people did, indeed, forge lies against me, I was not without fault.

God is good, and I needed to be reminded that He truly has done many good things for me. And the suffering was good because God's discipline is good. God's discipline brought me back to His Word. And His Word is more valuable than millions in gold and silver.

What a profound mystery to recognize that the most faithful, passionate followers of Jesus have been wounded deeply.

Be still in the pain

Joni Eareckson Tada is an artist, author, and speaker who, at the age of 17, dove into shallow water, rendering her a quadriplegic. Her struggle with depression, faith, and pain has inspired many. In her book, *A Place of Healing: Wrestling with the Mysteries of Suffering, Pain and God's Sovereignty*, she wrote "He has chosen not to heal me, but to hold me. The more intense the pain, the closer His embrace."[2]

The way God embraced me in my most intense pain was through His Word. I got to know Him there, and knowing Him allowed me to feel both the intensity of my pain and the closeness of His arms.

When the weight of your wait feels too heavy to bear, and you don't know if you can survive another day in the desert, God will show compassion. My encouragement for you is this: let the desert create a thirst for His Word. Do not abandon Him when it appears that following Him has brought more trouble. Allow the burden in your life to push you into the embrace of the Father. Read His Word even when you can't bear to hear it. Pray even when you don't know what to say.

"Jesus, I don't even know what to pray right now, I just need help," is a completely legitimate prayer. I have prayed it many times. Staying connected to Him is what matters—not the words that come out. With that as your map, you will find His heart.

Chapter Five

The Last Word

Moses cried, "let my people go!" And Pharaoh's stone heart was met with disaster upon disaster. The Nile and all their water turned to blood, frogs took over their homes, bowls, streets, and beds, gnats swarmed every inch of breathable air.

When the first plagues came, God allowed them to affect everyone, Egyptians and Hebrews alike. He even allowed the magicians in Egypt to mirror His work for a short time. The God of the Hebrews appeared weak and cruel. Weak compared to Egypt's gods who replicated plagues with apparent ease, and cruel to have His own people suffering along with the Egyptians. God was setting a precedent of pain for all the people in Egypt and Israel. But regardless of what they thought of Him, they could not deny that some god was active. The first three plagues got everyone's attention. I imagine every mother, father, son, and daughter was asking "Why is this happening? How do we make this stop? What god is doing this to us?" The plagues caused pain and loss, but every human being was looking to the heavens for an answer. The answer came in a swarm of flies.

God sent flies to cover Egypt. A merchant choked on an inhale of insects. A woman couldn't hang her laundry to dry before every inch of fabric was covered in black, swarming bodies. But the land where the Hebrew slaves lived was clear of flies. Finally, God was setting His people apart. "Then you will know that I am the Lord and that I am present even in the heart of your land," He said (Ex. 8:22b). He wanted His people to know He was present *with* them. And He wanted Egypt to see *whose God* was orchestrating these events.

From then on, Egypt continued to be ravaged, but the people of Israel were spared. Livestock died, people were covered in painful boils, hail pummeled anything under the open sky, and locusts swarmed and destroyed anything that survived the hail. Darkness covered the land so one couldn't see their own hand in front of their face, but the sun still shone in Goshen, where Israel lived. It was undeniable. Yahweh, the God of Israel, was in charge.

"Name a price that would excite you." It was an offer unlike anything we had received before, and the deal was as good as done.

In the autumn of 2021, I (Mike) was given an opportunity to speak about my book, *Thrown Off Script*. One attendee was so affected by the talk, he reached out to me immediately and started making plans for me to speak at his company's annual meeting. And money was no object.

In my mind, this was God's sign to embark on a career as a speaker! God was finally filling the holes in my work and ministry. I felt like a young Moses, connecting the dots to conclude this was indeed the God-ordained time to step into my purpose!

Then, out of the blue, the company canceled their regular, annual event. It felt like a rug was pulled out from under me. I grasped at air trying to find a place to land. No amount of phone calls or emails could kickstart this speaking career. Instead of launching my new life as a speaker, that "no" ushered us into years of unprecedented "silence."

We have experienced more canceled contracts, more abandoned proposals, more unanswered emails than seems reasonable for a pair of creative professionals to receive. We did the sad math: by the end of the following spring, around $80,000 worth of unprecedented proposals, agreements, and gigs had evaporated.

The *no's* were painful for a while until they were so frequent and expected, we became numb. To dull the pain of *no,* we tried not to hope at all.

But as devastating as all those *no's* were, they made God's *yesses* all the more evident. *Yesses* we previously would not have recognized as God being at work have shone bright like the sun over Goshen. Receiving a reply to an email, for example, seems mundane to most people. And it probably is. But since so many of our reach outs have gone unanswered, any email that is met with a favorable response is a clear marker that God is opening doors.

Reading a reply from an email or hearing encouragements for our ministry are like bright orange life rafts in a dark sea of *no's.* If we had received a *yes* to every effort, we would not notice the miracle of a *yes* when it did eventually come. God allowed a precedent of pain and disappointment so that when He *was* moving on our behalf, we would know He was with us, and could serve as an example that God was really in charge.

God proved Himself to be the One True God over the gods of the Egyptians by the power of His might through the first nine plagues. He decided the result; He chose where each would fall and who would be affected. There was no escape for His enemies. Everyone in Egypt knew who was in charge—from Pharaoh's palace to the smallest shack in Goshen. Even His own people were afflicted or saved based on His will alone.

And yet, the final plague was not delivered the same way. God, the unparalleled military strategist, employed a different tactic in the ultimate plague. The final trial came with a choice to make. God was going to strike down the firstborn male of every family, human and animal, Egyptian and Hebrew. I wonder if Moses thought God was being poetic in Exodus 4:22. "This is what the Lord says: Israel is my firstborn son. I commanded you, 'Let my son go, so he can worship me.' But since you have refused, I will now kill your firstborn son!" God was not speaking metaphorically. This was a very real consequence.

The choice for every inhabitant was simple. Believe God meant what He said, slaughter a lamb or goat and spread its blood on their doorposts, and ensure safety for your firstborn. Or, choose to ignore God, go about your day as usual, and wake up to a nightmare.

The Hebrews gathered in their homes that fateful night as the angel of death came. Those who believed He would do what He said He would do, and obeyed His instructions, held their sons in the morning. Everyone else mourned the sudden, unstoppable death of their firstborn. Everyone had the choice. Hebrew and Egyptian. But only the Hebrews obeyed. "Pharaoh and all his officials and all the Egyptians got up during the night, and there was loud wailing in Egypt, for there was not a house without someone dead" (Ex. 12:30).

Obeying God doesn't mean you're better *than* anyone else, but it certainly means you're better *off*.

Be still in the tension

Egyptians and Hebrews alike witnessed God flexing through the ten plagues. The particularly observant Hebrew may have collected some insights about God's heart through the process:

- Just because you are God's people doesn't mean you are exempt from pain and difficulty, *yet*, obeying God is better than ignoring Him.

- God is deadly serious about emphasizing his superiority over any other worshipped thing, *yet*, while God brings judgment, He always offers a way out for anyone who wants it.

- God sees you and wants to act on your behalf, *yet* He doesn't act in your timing and expectations.

That word *yet* is a hinge in each of those truths about God's heart. *Yet* carries the weight of truth on both sides. "This" is true, *yet*, "this" *also* has to be true. *Yet* is a word of tension. It seems like both sides can't coexist, *yet* they are both true at the same time. To follow God is to become familiar with tension. You've probably felt it in your time in the desert. A good deal of your frustration has probably revolved around the fact that you have to contend with two seemingly opposite things about God.

TO FOLLOW GOD IS TO BECOME FAMILIAR WITH TENSION.

As you wrestle with the tensions of God's protection and pain, judgment and mercy, and care and sovereignty, we encourage you to respond with a tension of your own. It comes from a man named Job,

who was forced to contend with a loving God who allowed unrelenting pain.

> "Though he slay me, yet
> will I hope in him" (Job
> 13:15, NIV).

God may go so far as to slay me. *Yet.* Yet I will choose to trust Him anyway.

It may be tough to swallow, but God has the last word. He holds the right to do whatever He wants in your life. Whatever desert He leads you to, whatever pain you face — He is the rightful owner of your life. He will work what's best for *Him*, and that doesn't always equate to what you think is best for *you*. He wants to establish his superiority over sin in your life. The process may hurt. He knows how to best utilize your life for His Kingdom. It may not be your plan. Yet ... will you hope in Him?

Chapter Six

The Long Way

If the Hebrew slaves had preserved any knowledge of geography over their 400 years in slavery, I bet they left Egypt and excitedly looked to the northeast, the shortest route to the Promised Land. Imagine their bewilderment when Moses turned his blinker on and headed south, per the Lord's instructions.

I can hear them argue, "that way will take so much longer. We're mere *days* away from the Promised Land. Let's go, Moses! There's nothing in the desert."

An elderly man leans on his staff and chimes in. "My friends, I went that way once to trade my master's papyrus and linen for cedar from Lebanon. On that route, the Philistines are violent."

"Philistines shmilistines!" A boy declares as he punches the air. "We can take 'em! I'll punch them in the face!"

"Yea!" The crowd cries out, "we have waited long enough for the Promised Land, let's not delay any longer!"

I truly wonder how much conversation was had about the route. If a husband and wife cannot agree on whether to take the highway or the back roads to the lake (an example that may or may not be pulled from personal experience), then I imagine a nation of people would not easily agree on how to get to the place God promised.

Exhausted from the weeks of plagues, adrenaline dying after the miraculous walk out of slavery, and irritated with this new leader, the former slaves followed Moses on a route that didn't make sense to them.

The clock rudely reminded me how dire my situation was. Two o'clock in the morning. I (Kelsey) was wandering the hall outside my bedroom. Tears and snot streamed down my face as I braced myself on the wall for support. The pain in my left leg was so severe, I couldn't sleep; I hadn't slept for a week.

"God, please, I need you to help me!" It is the deepest lament I have felt.

The pain started a week earlier when it shot down my hip and woke me out of a dead sleep. It was December 3rd, my 40th birthday. In a short amount of time, the pain overtook the entire left side of my leg, accompanied by numbness and weakness.

Soon, I couldn't walk. By the time December 25th came, I couldn't even sit to eat Christmas dinner with my family. The calendar turned a page, but I didn't. I spent the first three weeks of the new year laying flat on my back, starting at the ceiling. I was forced to cancel speaking engagements. I couldn't visit the hospital to hold my friend's newborn baby. I missed watching my daughter win her school spelling bee.

The diagnosis was a rupture to a herniated disc in my lumbar spine. The answer was steroids or surgery. Maybe both. The recovery would be lengthy and required months of physical therapy to learn to trust my body again.

The pain affected me physically, yes, but the even greater pain was the three-month interruption to my life. I mourned financial, social, and emotional losses and experienced mental, physical, and spiritual exhaustion that was difficult to bear.

This all happened the month I was planning to finish writing this book. Prior to this spine episode, I believed this month would be a pivotal season in our lives, for the better. After years of feeling stuck, the autumn of 2025 *finally* felt like we had a clear path forward. I remember being so excited to turn the big 4-0. I was telling everyone "Forty will be my best decade yet!" It felt like being free from Egypt and on my way to the Promised Land!

I thought we were ready to move full speed ahead toward our future. But God laid me flat on my back in a delay I didn't see coming. And it would be a long time before I recovered. God had brought us out of one season of pain and I truly thought we were about to find the long-awaited direct route to the life we long for. But God had another longer, roundabout delay planned.

When Pharaoh finally let the people go, God did not lead them along the main road that runs through Philistine territory, even though that was the shortest route to the Promised Land. God said, "If the people are faced with a battle, they might change their minds and return to Egypt." So God led them in a roundabout way through the wilderness toward the Red Sea (Ex. 13:17-18).

Remember, Exodus isn't a novel written to surprise and delight readers with twists and turns. It was written by Moses while he traveled the desert to remind people of who God is and what He had done. We'll discuss the Red Sea episode in more detail next chapter, but here's a consideration for now.

When verse 18 teases that God led the people "toward the Red Sea," it isn't with a sense of "ooooh… what's going to happen at the Red Sea?" It's written as a reminder to the readers that when God led them on a roundabout way, seemingly away from their destination, delaying their arrival, He was leading them toward the Red Sea—a dazzling display of God's faithfulness to His people, His salvation, His judgement, His power. This reminder comes up again in Numbers, Joshua, Isaiah, several Psalms, Hebrews, and 1 Corinthians.

The roundabout way became a landmark. Every testimony became a reminder of not only the pain of delay, but the God who made a way.

I don't know what your delay is. And as I write this, I don't even know how my herniated disc will be turned into a story for God's glory. The Hebrews didn't know where their long roundabout trip would take them, but you do have one thing the Hebrews didn't have: hindsight.

You can read the story of the Jews in the wilderness and understand that the same God who led them "to the Red Sea" is leading you somewhere, too. And using that hindsight, you can endure your unexpected delays a little differently. You can walk ahead with the trust that He is good, His plans are good, and His outcomes are what is best for you.

That is not to say it's easy to not know the outcomes. On the contrary, these God-ordained delays are some of the most challenging and confusing.

Not arriving

Wandering in the wilderness, stopped, camping out in the desert feels like the opposite of *arriving*. Whatever your goal, putting off arrival is discouraging, painful, and exhausting.

I certainly felt that way when my disc herniated. Laying on the couch unable to work for two months felt like the *opposite* of finishing this book. Instead of writing, I was weeping. Instead of planning for our future, I was planted on the couch. The excitement of a new phase of life was replaced with depression and inability to see any future at all. That delay is heartbreaking and it certainly doesn't make sense.

But what if God is taking the long way to *ensure* you arrive? Yes, the delay you're experiencing and I am experiencing feel like they're putting off the life we thought God had promised. But regardless of how the map looked, the long way through the wilderness was not the opposite of arriving for the Hebrews. Going back to Egypt would have been the opposite of arriving. By taking the long route, God was giving them their very best shot at actually stepping foot in the Promised Land instead of turning back to slavery.

When our family plays board games, and we do often, we pick up our pieces and we put them in the places on the board to bring about a win. When she's struggling to get ahead, sometimes our daughter will playfully put her piece at the victory line and say, "I win!"

Sometimes, I want God to pick me up like a little game piece and place me at the end of the game where I win at life. But, dear reader, you are not a meeple. And God is too kind to let you skip the delays. Getting you to the end as quickly as possible is not what is best for you. In a board game, the fun is in the decision making and problem solving along the way. Learning the game, appreciating the designer's skill, and spending time with the people we love. Your life is not all about the finish line. There are challenges that shape you, decisions that change you, problems that draw you closer to Jesus as you lean on Him in the struggle. And so, because He is good and kind toward you, He invites you into deserts of delay. He designs roundabout journeys during which He will show you more of who He is and reveal to you who you were created to be.

This is what God promises to each of us as we walk through our roundabout detours; "trust in the Lord with all your heart and lean not on your own understanding; in all your ways submit to him, and he will make your paths straight" (Proverbs 3:5-6).

This well-known proverb does not say "he will make your paths *short*." A quick result is not often what is best for us. So, He makes our paths long to give plenty of time to know Him while we walk.

KNOWING HIM LEADS TO TRUSTING HIM.

What this proverb *does* promise is that the path will be straight *if* we submit to Him. That condition on the promise matters. We're prone to make decisions and plans for our life based on what we see and know—our own understanding. However, God is unseen. Faith is believing what you cannot see. Our own understanding is limited by our senses. To live a truly unlimited life, we need to trust Him who is unseen. That's what the long delays offer—the opportunity to know Him and experience Him in the seasons when our senses are saying "nothing makes sense." It is there that we move past what makes sense, and into what builds trust. Knowing Him leads to trusting Him. And trusting Him turns wild, untamed, crooked wilderness into straight paths.

Avoiding a fight

The long way granted the people of God more time to know God and would ensure they made it to the Red Sea where God had something awesome to show them. But there was another reason God didn't take the shortest route to the Promised Land. God led the people the long way to avoid Philistine territory. He knew "If the people are faced with a battle, they might change their minds and return to Egypt" (Ex. 13:17).

But hold on, what a minute—God sent hailstones on Egypt. *Egypt!* The world's superpower was brought to its knees by the God of Abraham. Why would He avoid Philistines? Couldn't He just do the same thing to them that He'd done in Egypt? One death angel could wipe them out in one swoop!

Have you ever prayed, "God, you've done this before, do it again!"

Has He ever ... not?

Sometimes I wonder if we think we have God figured out. When we witness Him work, when we see a miracle, when a prayer gets answered. If we're honest, can we admit that our minds think, "Oh, okay, so that's how He works." Then a "next time" happens, and we think, "I know how to get out of this. God! Do that thing you did before!"

I'll admit I've done this. I've prayed for people to be healed and seen with my own eyes as pain and chronic conditions left their bodies. So, I prayed in the same way for myself, expecting God to do the same thing with my herniated disc as I'd seen Him do with a woman's neuropathy in her hands: heal. Immediately.

He didn't. And I was overwhelmingly discouraged.

May I propose something? Perhaps we don't have God figured out.

You have a God who knows the best strategy for every battle you will face. More than that, He knows your limitations. He is not restricted by them, but He knows when to stop pushing them. Sometimes He sends plagues on your enemies; other times, He'll guide you away from the fight altogether.

Since Moses arrived in Egypt, the Hebrews had been pushed harder by their slave drivers, they had been personally affected by three devastating plagues, they had seen what the God of their ancestors was capable of, and saw He was even willing to take the life of firstborn sons of those who don't obey Him.

It was a lot.

God knew their limits. God knew if Israel was faced with an attack too soon in their journey, they would want to go back to what was known. He loved them too much to take them on a quick route with encounters that would send them running back to Egypt.

There are times we want God to fight; we want to see a display of His power. But certainly God can get just as much glory for avoiding a fight as He can for winning it. It's not weakness. It's wisdom. On the other hand, there are times we want God to take us on a detour; we'd like to avoid challenges and pain. But God may say it's time for hailstones, so He can show you He is your strength and protection even when the odds are stacked against you.

In either case, we have to recognize we don't have the full picture, but we can trust the One who does.

Be still in the "why?"

"Why is this happening? How do we make it stop?" We've prayed that prayer and we're willing to bet you have, too. The 2:00am prayer crawl in my hallway was one of those times. I pleaded with God, "please God, make this pain stop. I can't live like this!"

"Why do bad things happen to good people?"

"How could a good God allow such evil in the world?"

"Why me? Why is this pain and suffering happening to me?"

These questions stem from a belief that we know what's best and God's not doing His job. We think we ought to be in charge. After all, if we *were* in charge, things would be different. As author and podcaster Allie Beth Stuckey often says, "people think they're nicer than God."[3]

When we ask, "why is this happening?" we might as well be demanding, "God, this is not how I would do things, you owe me an explanation!"

When we put it that way it seems silly, right? It's laughable to think that the Lord owes us any explanation for how He chooses to bring about His plans in the world.

The victory is always God's. As we get to know Him, we will learn to trust Him even when it doesn't make sense. When we can't see rhyme or reason behind what He allows in this world, we can learn to trust that He is in control. We can stop questioning God at every turn.

Part of knowing God's heart in your delay is trusting He has a plan and a purpose. After all, "we know that in all things God works for the good of those who love him, who have been called according to his purpose" (Romans 8:28). But oftentimes, that verse is misused to say "the good" will be our definition of "good." But God's definition of "good" will not always make sense, and it will not *feel* good all the time. He knows what's best. Sometimes that includes a considerable amount of pain.

Like trusting my physical therapist even when the movement hurts, what is "good" comes as a result of what hurts most. It's good not because it's pain free, but because it's the path toward what is best for us.

Rewriting stories

Recovering from a spine injury does not happen overnight. Pushing too hard, too fast, would have landed me in the hospital worse off than I was before. The path forward through this delay is trusting my physical therapist to push me slowly, with intentionality, so I can heal. Muscles atrophied during months of immobility due to pain. They need to work for me to regain independence. That work is uncomfortable, but I know every press-up and squat is building a foundation of health.

Along this delay, I have also learned to rewrite a story in my life. For multiple decades, I have believed I "have a bad back." It's what I was told by a chiropractor when I was in my early teens, and it's an identity I have carried since. After all, he had the X-ray to prove it!

Then I got an MRI.

Since being examined by two trained spine surgeons who look at MRIs every day, I have heard three times, "that's a good back" (You know, other than the messed up disc part).

This long, horrible delay turned out to be a rediscovery. I am not a girl "with a bad back." I am a person who needs to improve core strength and posture—but I am not a victim of my skeleton. I am learning to trust that my body has capabilities I had written off for most of my life. I have learned to believe my body isn't irrevocably broken; I can get stronger and be free of the pain that has been a constant for thirty years.

Without this disc rupturing into my spinal column, I wouldn't have had this opportunity to rewrite my pain story. I would have continued to be angry at my body for lacking structural integrity. Now, I work through physical therapy with a new vision for my future. Not only will this leg pain end, but I will also appreciate the body God gave me in a way that had been hindered before by stories of "a bad back." I am relearning how I think about my body, how I talk about my body, and what I believe is possible in this body.

The Hebrews also had stories to rewrite: "we are slaves," "we are despised," "we are forgotten by God." These are identity-shaping stories. Every aspect of life was shaped by these beliefs about themselves and God. Such stories would not sustain them as a nation if they arrived at their destination too quickly. Can you imagine walking into the Promised Land and trying to chase out the occupants under the identity of "despised slaves?" A people "forgotten by God" would easily be intimidated and overrun by the occupants in the land and bullied out of their God-given promise. The long, roundabout way through the wilderness was a time to re-write their stories. To learn who they were, and who God really was. To relearn how they thought of themselves, how they spoke as nation, and what they believed was possible with God.

What stories are part of your identity? Perhaps you're aware of them. Perhaps, like me, you won't uncover your identity stories until you're faced with a painful delay. Can I encourage you to pray right now? Ask God what stories you believe about yourself that simply aren't true. Don't delay. This is the end of this chapter. Put the book down and pray. Ask God to rewrite your stories so you can realign your self image to the image God gave you: His.

Chapter Seven

The Sea

As Egypt faded in the rear view mirror, via the long way, the Israelites soon approached the shore of the Red Sea. This route made such little human sense, even Pharaoh scratched his head! We have his amusement recorded in the story, "The Israelites are confused. They are trapped in the wilderness!" (Exodus 14:3)

We have had our share of onlookers give their advice on how we *ought* to be living. One well-meaning friend suggested, "Just get a job at Home Depot and make some money while you figure out your 'ministry' thing." That would make sense. But God didn't tell us to get a job at Home Depot. God told us to stand firm and keep trusting Him even when nothing makes sense.

Such advice has made us feel very alone. A handful of people have heard our story and encouraged us to continue. Others minimally mask their opinion that we're being foolish or irresponsible, and our faith in this area is uncomfortable to them.

When you take the long way, people will be watching how you follow God. They'll see you take longer than they think you should.

They'll see you stopped and camped out instead of hustling through difficult situations. And like Pharaoh, they might call you "confused and trapped."

God led the Israelites the long way so they wouldn't face war with the Philistines, yes. But that didn't mean they wouldn't encounter resistance. In fact, God knew they would have enemies hot on their trail. He planned it that way.

"I have planned this in order to display my glory through Pharaoh and his whole army. After this the Egyptians will know that I am the Lord!... When my glory is displayed through them, all Egypt will see my glory and know that I am the Lord!" (Ex. 14:4,18).

God wanted His own people to grow to know Him. He also wanted the Egyptians to know who He was. He will call you to crazy hard places so that the people watching you, following you, criticizing your faith will see how He fights for you and they, too, will know He is the Lord.

Pharaoh chased after the Israelites with 600 chariots, all his horses, and all of Egypt's troops. God led His people to the edge of the Red Sea, and Pharaoh's army pursued, catching up with them at the shore.

Israel couldn't go forward; there was an impassable sea in the way. They couldn't go around it; their pursuers would cut them off and cut them down. They couldn't turn back; the bridge was burned and their previous slave drivers were cornering them with no intention of letting them escape. They were trapped.

Exodus 14:10 records the Hebrews' fear. "As Pharaoh approached, the people of Israel looked up and panicked when they saw the Egyptians overtaking them. They cried out to the Lord, and they said to Moses, 'Why did you bring us out here to die in the wilderness?

Weren't there enough graves for us in Egypt? What have you done to us? Why did you make us leave Egypt? Didn't we tell you this would happen while we were still in Egypt? We said, "Leave us alone! Let us be slaves to the Egyptians. It's better to be a slave in Egypt than a corpse in the wilderness!"'"

I echo their despair. I am the Israelites crying out from slavery in Egypt: "God, please bring me out of the way of this world! Give us a life of ministry and closeness with you!" Then He does exactly that, and I am too quickly the Israelites by the Red Sea bemoaning, "God, I don't see how I can go forward like this! I'm scared, and it's hard! It would have been easier if we could just live like everyone else!"

It's easy to minimize the negatives of the past and maximize the negatives of the present. When we focus on the circumstances, our memories trick us and our imaginations scare us. Our memories tell us what we escaped wasn't *that* bad. And our imaginations tell us our future is hopeless. When we focus on our circumstance, it pulls us away from our relationship with God, which has been—and continues to be—His main priority. The antidote to this anguish is knowing God's heart for relationship.

OUR MEMORIES TRICK US AND OUR IMAGINATIONS SCARE US.

We have the benefit of thousands of years of hindsight from the Bible about the heart and character of God and we still forget. The Israelites didn't have all that experience to lean on. That generation only knew what they saw in Egypt, and a couple of stories about a handful of patriarchs. His display of power in Egypt brought up the same questions they had during His silence.

Is God even real?

Is God with us here or not?

Is God good?

He destroyed the Egyptians' livestock and way of life. Will He provide for His people?

He covered the land in darkness. Will He light their path moving forward?

He took life. Will He preserve theirs?

Sure, they were slaves in Egypt. Are they slaves now to this God who proved Himself stronger than the Egyptian gods?

For hundreds of years, He was their cultural God in the stories of Abraham, Isaac, and Jacob. He was the one they kept their traditions for, and even prayed to, but they didn't know He listened, or cared, or wanted a relationship. This is a problem that is still relevant today: God's people didn't really know God.

We know *about* Him. We sing praises for Him. We pray to Him. But do you *know* Him?

Do you settle for a faith that informs you or are you willing to let it interrupt you?

Is Jesus your Sunday morning savior but a Monday morning afterthought?

God broadcast in Egypt, "Hey! Those are my people!" And now, at the shore of the Red Sea, He brought them into an impossible situation where He could show off and teach them more about Himself, so they could say, "Hey! That's our God!"

There's a difference between being God's people, and God being their God. It's two-sided, and it's the relationship God had been craving all along.

Be still and watch

When I (Kelsey) become particularly discouraged, unsure if I can keep walking this path of faith, most often God's response to me is to not do anything drastic. Most often, His gentle kindness to me is to say, "Don't be afraid. Just stand still and watch the Lord rescue you." Through a conversation, Bible reading, a sermon, or a song, God reaches down into my complaining, fearful heart, and says, "Child, stop striving. Keep trusting. Do nothing and watch me be God."

We humans appreciate when there's a bold move to make. We like the story of pulling ourselves up by the bootstraps and standing on our own two feet. We love independence and self-sufficiency. Getting ourselves out of a bind can be thrilling. We enjoy maintaining control over our lives and finding a way forward by our own cleverness and hard work.

I think that's exactly why when I seek Him, He tells me to stop and watch. I can't see Him be God if I'm calling all the shots. I will never see His miracles if I'm pushing my agenda. I won't witness *His* greatness if *I* am working every angle.

God led His people to the shore of the Red Sea where they felt trapped. A miracle was the only way out. When Israel was trapped at the Red Sea, they couldn't go back to Egypt, but they couldn't move forward, God had one message for them:

"Don't be afraid. *Just stand still and watch the Lord* rescue you today. The Egyptians you see today will never be seen again. The Lord himself will fight for you. Just stay calm" (Ex. 14:13-14 emphasis added).

God Himself provided a way out of impossible circumstances—circumstances God was responsible for in the first place! He pushed His people to their most extreme limits so that the rescue was in God's hands and His hands alone.

When He leads you to circumstances that are beyond your limits of faith, comfort, and understanding, go with Him. He shows up in those impossible places to do what only He can do.

We know how things ended at the Red Sea. Moses waved his hand over the waters of the sea, and a strong wind blew all night creating a dry path with walls of water on both sides.

Israel crossed over the Red Sea on dry ground. When the Egyptians tried to follow, the water came crashing back down and every soldier and horse died in the deluge. All this for God's ongoing purpose of proving to His people that He is their God, He is for them, and He fights for them.

"When the people of Israel saw the mighty power that the Lord had unleashed against the Egyptians, they were filled with awe before him. They put their faith in the Lord and in his servant Moses" (Ex. 14:31).

Perhaps the obstacle you're facing right now is not something to get around or work through. Perhaps, the obstacle is there so you will stop and recognize your inability to move past it on your own. Our obstacles are opportunities for us to know God more by stopping. When God brings you to the shore of impossible, He is inviting you to see Him do what only He can do. When God leads you beyond your capacity, you have an opportunity to trust Him to make a way through.

God loves showing His people and their enemies who He is. His strategies haven't changed. He is orchestrating events and circumstances in your life to show you who He is and to show those watching you that He is the one, true God. *To them, your confidence looks like confusion. But to God, your tenacity looks like trust.*

Chapter Eight

The Provision

I f Exodus was a movie, the Red Sea crossing would be the triumphant ending, and this song would play under the credits:

> *You will bring them in and plant them*
> *on the mountain of your inheritance—*
> *the place, Lord, you made for your dwelling,*
> *the sanctuary, Lord, your hands established.*
> *The Lord reigns for ever and ever.*
> (Ex. 15:18)

Riding the high of the previous display of God's power, Moses and his sister, Miriam, sang this song recapping God's victory, and prophesying the coming fulfillment of His promise. They predicted the fall of the pagan nations ahead of them, and praised God for what He had done and would do.

But Exodus isn't a movie. It was real life, and crossing the Red Sea was far from the end. While Miriam's song was still stuck in their heads...

> Moses led the people of Israel away from the Red Sea, and they moved out into the desert of Shur. They traveled in this desert for three days without finding any water. When they came to the oasis of Marah, the water was too bitter to drink. So they called the place Marah (which means "bitter").
>
> Then the people complained and turned against Moses. "What are we going to drink?" they demanded. (Ex. 15:22-24)

It only took three days before the people complained. They witnessed one of the most jaw-dropping miracles of all time, but still didn't trust God. It's painfully relatable. *Just because God came through in one area doesn't mean we believe He'll come through in another.*

The people were bitter. Bitter like the water at Marah.

God knew what they needed and directed Moses' attention to a log. When Moses threw the log into the water, the water changed. Some translations say the water became "drinkable." But the New King James Version says, "the waters were made sweet" (Ex. 15:22-25). God didn't simply make the bitter water "good enough." He made it sweet. He turned what was bitter and unusable into sweetness that satisfied.

I (Kelsey) have some of the most beautiful friends. Inside and out, yes, but I'm thinking of the surface-level sense of the word. They look like full-on models just walking around on the earth like they're one of us. But they're also kind, generous, smart, and funny. One of these women loves to shop. I remember one summer where she was wearing a new dress every Sunday at church. I would get so envious. I never buy new clothes, primarily because I can't afford to buy new clothes.

I never thought of myself as materialistic. But, when the Lord led us into this financial desert and every dollar He provided was spoken for by rent or bills or necessities, I realized how much unnecessary stuff I really *wanted* to buy. I'd mock commercials parading this season's new styles to convince you to update your wardrobe. But then, I'd look at my dresses when the weather turned warm and think, "I really do want new clothes that are more fashionable." I would scoff at women who never seemed satisfied with their clothes, but when the weather turned cold, I would wish I could drop a few hundred dollars on new, seasonal sweaters.

I was bitter. Like the water at Marah.

But through the drought of not being able to buy whatever I want, the Lord has retrained my heart to *want* less. I learned the difference between the bitterness of wanting what I can't have, and the contentment found in not wanting what I don't have.

God surprises me in fun ways now. One day, I was looking at my closet, preparing for an anniversary trip with Mike. I really wished I could have something new to wear. Not bitter, just asking my Heavenly Father for something new to wear.

That week, I went to church and received a gift! My pastor's mother-in-law loves HSN, the Home Shopping Network, and had bought a little outfit that she thought looked cute on the model. Well, it didn't fit her right, and her daughter, my pastor's wife, thought of me. It fit me perfectly, and God gave me a new outfit to wear on my anniversary trip. (A trip He also paid for, by the way).

What once was a bitter resentment of new clothes and envy for what I didn't have has been turned into contentment. And I have the pleasure of experiencing the sweetness of the Lord giving me good gifts like a new outfit. I no longer look at my friend's wardrobe with disdain. I am genuinely happy for her when she spins into church in a new dress because I'm genuinely happy with what I have. And her hand-me-downs? So cute!

> It was there at Marah that the Lord set before them the following decree as a standard to test their faithfulness to him. He said, "If you will listen carefully to the voice of the Lord your God and do what is right in his sight, obeying his commands and keeping all his decrees, then I will not make you suffer any of the diseases I sent on the Egyptians; for I am the Lord who heals you" (Ex. 15:25-26).

At Marah, an incredible thing happened. God gave His people a new name by which to call him: "the Lord who heals" or Yahweh Rapha. "Yahweh" they knew from the burning bush, but "Yahweh Rapha" was a new revelation of who God is and His heart for His people.

The God who heals

I used to think of Yahweh Rapha as the God who heals sickness. And He is, in that God does heals sickness. But the name Yahweh Rapha was given to the people at Marah, where He turned a necessity from bitter to sweet. If we limit our understanding of Yahweh Rapha to being a glorified physician, we miss a larger truth.

To uncover it, let's get personal. What has been a point of bitterness in your walk through the desert? What has been the target of your complaints? What lack makes you feel discontent?

Part of what made Marah an even more bitter experience is the fact that it was water—the most essential human need! Come on God, it's not like I'm mad that I don't have a Lamborghini. I just thought you'd at least take care of my basic needs! I'm not asking for a mansion, I just need to pay rent. I'm not asking to walk the red carpet, I just want to walk to the bathroom without pain!

How much does God have to provide before I'm not bitter?

Is my faith only going so far as my needs are being met?

These questions sting me to even write them. But God is interested in the answers. Of course, He knows them, and wants you to know Him as more than the God who provides your basic needs, or heals your temporary body.

Like making bitter water drinkable, Yahweh Rapha underwent the work of healing the deep bitterness in His people's hearts, every fear and trauma that poisoned them against their God.

The Lord wants to heal more than your cold or cancer. Can He heal those things? Yes. Might He? I hope so. But beyond that, He wants to heal what is poisoned, bitter, and doesn't give life. Yahweh Rapha heals all that is broken and makes it sweet.

Manna

Within the week Israel complained again. "'If only the Lord had killed us back in Egypt,' they moaned. 'There we sat around pots filled with meat and ate all the bread we wanted. But now you have brought us into this wilderness to starve us all to death'" (Ex. 16:3).

It would be easy to say, "why do they keep complaining? They're free from slavery and should be grateful!" But they weren't free yet—not really. Yes, their bodies were no longer chained in Egypt, but they weren't yet free from the mindset of slavery. They were not free as the people of God, because they didn't know themselves as anything but slaves.

God knew this. He provided.

> Then the Lord said to Moses, "I have heard the Israelites' complaints. Now tell them, 'In the evening you will have meat to eat, and in the morning you will have all the bread you want. Then you will know that I am the Lord your God" (Ex. 16:11-12).

When the people were hungry, he sent bread from heaven called *manna*. *Manna* literally means "what is it?" because they did not know what it was. But they were able to collect the flakes that collected after the dew evaporated and make it into bread. God also sent quails for meat to eat (Ex. 16:1-26). Quails upon quails upon quails.

He wanted His people to know Him. Not only that, He wanted them to know Him as theirs. At the risk of sounding redundant, God's primary focus was relationship. He gave miraculous provision of bread and meat, He provided drinkable water, all so they would know Him as generous, healer, restorer, provider. He was intentionally helping His people shift from an identity of slave to sons. He was showing them that He was not like their captors in Egypt. He is not cruel, petty, greedy, and harsh. On the contrary, He is kind, substantive, and generous.

Mundane miracles

Manna felt like a miracle—once. That first day was undoubtedly filled with wonder and amazement. Celebration, even. The second day, slightly less so. By year thirty-seven, collecting manna felt more like a chore than a miracle. But is it any less a miracle when honey wafers materialize from heaven—*again*?

Collecting manna can be discouraging and painful. It's a daily reminder that you are still in the wilderness. Frankly, it's hard to be thankful for the constant reminder that you're not where you want to be, not where you used to be, and are dependent on someone else to get what you need.

We have come to call every one-off job or income earned from outside of our primary ministry as "manna." Mike painting a family member's deck? "Go get that manna!" Kelsey watching babies so their mom can run errands alone? "Thanks for picking up that manna!" What we call "manna" in our gig-based life is not the exciting, purpose-filled, Kingdom work we love. It's the mundane stuff we'd rather not do. Calling it "manna" reminds us that every dollar is from God—no matter how exciting the work was that earned it. It keeps us grateful and humble to see these mundane tasks as ways God is actively caring for us.

Manna is a miracle disguised as the mundane. God's provision isn't always flashy and fun. It may not feel like abundance. It can be repetitive. But how you view God's mundane provision is a direct reflection of your heart.

HOW YOU VIEW GOD'S MUNDANE PROVISION IS A DIRECT REFLECTION OF YOUR HEART.

Contentment, gratitude, and humility come from acknowledging the miracle. Discontentment, grumbling, and restlessness come from feeling let down by the mundane.

By providing for us in these "mundane miracles," God has healed the bitterness of discontent. He has healed the sickness of gluttony. He has freed us from the slavery of wanting what we don't need. He has shown us that we can live off of less than we think and still be happier than we thought possible. Manna has taught us to be content with what He gives and trust it's enough.

God provided daily miracles to provide for the people's daily needs. When they were thirsty again, God instructed Moses to strike a rock with his staff and water came pouring out (Ex. 17:1-6). Exodus 17:7 tells us that "Moses named the place Massah (which means 'test') and Meribah (which means 'arguing') because the people of Israel argued with Moses and tested the Lord by saying, "Is the Lord here with us or not?""

It was the same questions:

Is God real?

Is God with us here or not?

Is God good?

I Am answered with daily provision for their basic needs. Food and water became the currency of trust.

It seemed no matter how many times God provided for them, the next challenge they faced left them asking the same question, "Is the Lord here with us or not?" With every fear they faced, bitterness bloomed. Every unmet expectation was like a shot of a drug, poisoning their hearts and minds, telling them, "God is not good and doesn't care about you."

We have had our own days, weeks, months of *meribah* contention with God. We have fought with Him and said, "You're not doing enough!"

We have had our fair share of *massah* temptation to question where God is in all of this. "Did we hear right?" "Are we dumb?" And when we're painfully honest, "I think we'd provide for ourselves better than what God is doing right now."

Perhaps you don't live off of a gig-based income. You might have a salary or regular hours. But do you have any needs that aren't met the way you want them to be? Have you ever prayed for a miracle? Did you see that miracle come the way you wanted it? Did an answer come at the exact time you prayed for it? Did it ever feel late? Did it ever feel underwhelming?

By all means, keep praying these prayers. But if you feel disappointed and disillusioned because of unanswered prayers like we have, perhaps it's time to ask the question: What do we truly want most: what God can provide? or God Himself?

The best bread

It's probably in the top three most famous miracles of Jesus: feeding 5,000 families from a few loaves of bread and some fish. You'd think witnessing that miracle would inspire a wave of faith and devotion. And at first, it seemed like that might be the case. The next day, the crowds boarded several boats and crossed the sea of Galilee to look for Jesus in another seaside town. They tried to play it cool, "Oh! Hey! It's Jesus! Wow, what are the odds? Hey man, when did you get here?"

Jesus saw through them. He replied, "You want to be with me because I fed you, not because you understood the miraculous signs" (John 6:26).

"Well, we want to do God's work. Where should we start?"

Jesus was direct, but patient, "There's really only one thing God wants you to do: believe in me."

"Believe in you? Well, show us a miracle! You know, something like Moses did? Moses gave our ancestors bread in the wilderness. Can you do anything like that?"

You can almost feel Jesus' eyes roll. There were so many things wrong with that response. One single day after he literally, miraculously, provided bread for them! "First of all, Moses didn't give you manna. God did. Second, He's doing it again, except this time, He's offering you true bread."

"Great! We'd like some of that every day!"

I imagine Jesus practically shouting, "*I am* the bread of life! Whoever comes to *me* will never be hungry again!"

When the people asked for a miracle, they already had in mind what that would look like. They came to Jesus with an expectation for Him to meet. But Jesus had something way better, and totally different in mind. It looked less like conquest and provisions, and more like a cross and an empty tomb.

Sometimes our miracles look mundane because they don't meet our expectation of what a miracle should look like. Flashy miracles might get you on fire for a little while. But miracles don't sustain a relationship. Only Jesus sustains us.

In the time that followed, Jesus performed many more miracles. He raised people from the dead, healed the sick, turned water to wine, and walked on the sea. Some people today think their faith would be easier to hold onto if they saw miracles like that. But just like the Israelites complained three days after the Red Sea miracle, people in Jesus' life abandoned Him.

John 12:37 is one of the saddest verses in the Bible, "Despite all the miraculous signs Jesus had done, most of the people still did not believe in him."

It's easy to slap our foreheads at the crowd's responses to Jesus. I (Kelsey) certainly did, until I realized my prayers were painfully similar to theirs. I was increasingly focused on God's provision. There was a time I even fell into the trap of thinking if I could just get the right words in the right order for the right prayer—then God would do what I wanted Him to do. Mike had to confront me. "God's not holding your blessing hostage until you say the right thing. He might be missing spending time with you, though."

I had to be brutally honest and say my faith was bold enough to know He was willing and able to provide, but I had begun seeing Him as a means to an end. I was compelled by the truth that *He loved me and wanted to be with me, not for anything I could do for Him, but simply for who I was. Why was I not showing the same love to Him in return?*

We had to stop in the desert of delay. Stop being concerned with perishable things. Stop desiring what He could provide over who He is. Stop wanting Him to show up the way I expect before I trust Him.

Be still in the hunger

A truly hungry person will not decline a roast beef sandwich simply because they prefer turkey.

Are you hungry for God to do something? Are you hungry enough to let God provide whatever and however He wants? Are you hungry enough to pick up the provision He's sending from heaven, even if it's weird, uncomfortable, painful, or bland?

What in your life reminds you of manna? And then, the key question: What does manna remind you of? Does it remind you that you're not where you want to be? Or does it remind you that God sees you and cares for you every day? The result is either discontentment and grumbling, or contentment and gratitude.

Let this time in the desert create a hunger. When you get those hunger pains, what is your reaction? Do you get *hangry*?

Sometimes God allows us to be hungry and thirsty. If not literally, then financially. Relationally. Spiritually. If God's people in the wilderness can help us avoid learning the lesson the hard way, stop complaining today. Instead, gather the manna. Of course, that requires looking for it every day, trusting it'll be there when the morning dew evaporates. Instead of looking back to where you were and how good you had it, or looking forward to where you want to be, pick up your bread.

Notice what He is providing *today*.

Thank Him for His provision *today*.

Acknowledge that, even if it isn't what you want, you know God is providing what you need *today*.

Pray like Jesus taught:

> "This, then, is how you should pray:
> 'Our Father in heaven,
> hallowed be your name,
> your kingdom come,
> your will be done,
> on earth as it is in heaven.
> Give us today our daily bread.
> And forgive us our debts,
> as we also have forgiven our debtors.
> And lead us not into temptation,
> but deliver us from the evil one.'"
> (Matthew 6:9-13, NIV)

Chapter Nine

The Strength

So far, the Israelites' "freedom" was looking more like being pursued by an Egyptian horde, walking through the desert for days, and running out of food and water. Imagine their exhaustion and fear when they saw a dust cloud on the horizon, stirred up by the marching of angrily-approaching nomads.

Amalekites.

They were the Israelites' distant cousins—descendants of Jacob's wild brother Esau—and they obviously had a chip on their hairy shoulders. I don't know if the Amalekites came looking for a fight, or if it was an unpleasant coincidence, but either way, Moses and the Israelites needed this confrontation like a cat needs a swim lesson. Moses nodded to Joshua, his right hand man, to ready the fighting men. He grabbed the staff of God and prepared for battle.

Wait—I thought God said He was taking them the long way around so they could avoid battles! That's mostly true. But there's a big difference between taking the short route with guaranteed opposition, and taking the long, God-led route with God-approved trials. Ultimately, God knew what was reasonable to expect His people to be able to handle. And He knows your limitations, too.

"I don't think I can do this anymore," one tissue box down, and halfway into the second catching my tears and snot, I (Kelsey) told Mike, "I trust God. I do. I just don't know how much longer I can wait month to month for income. I don't know anymore if we're acting in faith or foolishness." Our 13-year-old daughter was paid $50 by her summer camp and had more in her bank account than we did.

It was a different despair. I can honestly say I wasn't complaining about manna, I wasn't leaning on my understanding, I wasn't questioning God. I fully believed He would take care of our needs. I was simply exhausted.

I felt like I didn't have the strength to keep pushing on. I didn't know how many more closed doors I could take. Everyone has a breaking point, and I'm confident I was on the brink of mine.

Flexing your faith muscle

Moses, staff in hand, called his brother, Aaron, and his friend, Hur, to follow him up a hill to watch over the battle. Picture the two armies in a valley: the horde of Amalekites on the left, brandishing sabers that glinted in the desert sun, and the ragtag group of former slaves on the right, swinging Egyptian swords they grabbed on their way out of town. We don't know how much God instructed Moses ahead of time, but I (Mike) like to imagine Moses accidentally discovered the secret to success in this battle:

He cheered, raising his staff above his head, "Let's go, Hebrews, let's go!" Aaron and Hur clapped in rhythm, and as they did, the dusty mass of Israelites shifted slightly to the left as they took some ground. "Yes! Hey Amalekites—you sons of Esau—you tired? You need some stew?" Moses put his staff down to give his friends a double-high five and a chest bump. That was a pretty sick ancestry-based burn. But their celebration waned when they saw the Israelite clump slide steadily back to the right. They were losing ground. "Josh!" Moses cupped his hands around his mouth to amplify his shouts to his man on the front lines. "Joshua! Sweep the leg!" But Joshua couldn't hear him. Moses picked up his staff again and began waving it over his head, trying to get Joshua's attention, and almost immediately, the embattled fray scurried to the left, in favor of the Israelites again.

Moses' eyes widened. He immediately straightened his elbows next to his ears and held the staff up as high as he could. Joshua's army scored more and more yards. Apparently the more his staff was above his head, the more the Israelites would win. We can do this! But as the day dragged on, so did the battle. Why was this taking so long? God was clearly involved; why couldn't He just end it already?

"Moses' arms soon became so tired he could no longer hold them up" (Ex. 17:12a).

Have you ever felt like you're doing the right thing, and you've been doing the right thing for a while, but the battle is still raging, and you're getting tired? It's confusing and exhausting. "I get it, God! I understand what you're doing! Can we be done now?" That's certainly how we felt.

Sometimes, waiting on God feels like suffering when we haven't done anything wrong. Peter offers God's perspective on patient endurance:

You get no credit for being patient if you are beaten for doing wrong. But if you suffer for doing good and endure it patiently, God is pleased with you. For God called you to do good, even if it means suffering, just as Christ suffered for you. He is your example, and you must follow in his steps (1 Peter 2:20-21).

Enduring makes you more like Jesus. And so, even when you feel like you've "learned your lesson," the real goal isn't the lesson *you've* pieced together. The goal is for you to be like Jesus and that result comes through endurance and suffering.

Well, that's not fun. No, it's not. But take courage.

Moses came to the end of his ability to endure the physical challenge of holding up the staff. Moses was tempted to quit. But, instead of God concluding the trial, He offered Moses new strength in the form of his friends. "So Aaron and Hur found a stone for him to sit on. Then they stood on each side of Moses, holding up his hands. So his hands held steady until sunset" (Ex. 17:12b).

This beautiful image inspires two solid takeaways for us.

First, we see a compelling example of the interplay between God's involvement in our trials, and our responsibility through them. The word "steady" is translated from the Hebrew word *emunah*—from which we get the word "amen"—and means "faithful." With the help of his friends, Moses' hands held *faithfully* until the sun went down. Faithfulness is not simply a state of mind. It's also a state of action. That's why James says faith without works is dead (James 2:26). But faithful action does not always look like going, running, and doing. It often means holding steady, straining under the weight until the battle is over. It's an active flexing of the faith muscle.

Second, it displays the value of surrounding yourself with like-minded friends who are willing to support you when you are weak. As they say, "a cord of three strands is not quickly broken" (Ecclesiastes 4:2, NIV).

It was summer, the hottest week of the year. That night was a midweek service at church. After the message, our church went into a time to pray together and encourage one another.

A friend came up to me (Kelsey) with a blessing for our family. "The curse is lifted," he said. My mind immediately went to what we have unaffectionately called the "abyss"—the place all our hopes and dreams (and unanswered emails) go to die. Hope jumped up out of nowhere that maybe our time of waiting was nearing its end. Maybe this battle through obscurity and brokenness was nearly won.

A few minutes later, another man spoke over us again—this time, with very specific encouragement. "I don't know what you've had to go through to be where you are, but the Lord wants you to know that you are right where you're supposed to be. You've had to give up a lot to be here, but God has been changing you and preparing you for something new."

He then sat at the piano and sang over us one line of Isaiah 61:3, "The garment of praise for the spirit of heaviness."

Sitting on the floor of our church, surrounded by people praying for us, receiving encouragement that could only come from the Holy Spirit, I knew I could keep going as long as it would take. Like Aaron and Hur, friends lifted my heavy, tired arms. But more importantly, they pointed me to Jesus and directed my focus on God.

On my own, I was feeble and pessimistic. Surrounded by others lifting my eyes to the Lord, I was filled with courage and hope for the first time in a long time.

The brave wait

We tend to think of waiting as something we're forced into. Nobody would choose to wait for something to happen. And if they did, it must be because they're scared. Wait and see what happens. Wait and see if someone else will do something instead. Waiting feels like a weak, stagnant thing to do. But Psalm 27:14 paints a different picture:

"Wait patiently for the Lord. Be brave and courageous. Yes, wait patiently for the Lord".

Apparently, when it comes to waiting for the Lord to do His work, patient waiting is far from weak and stagnant. It's brave and courageous. It's pedal-to-the-metal, money-where-your-mouth-is faith, and it's not for the faint of heart.

God understands the strength required to wait. That's why He offers this beautiful promise in an often-quoted passage in Isaiah:

"But those who wait on the Lord shall renew their strength; they shall mount up with wings like eagles, they shall run and not be weary, they shall walk and not faint" (Isaiah 40:31, NKJV).

This verse was taught in my (Mike's) Christian high school (whose mascot was, in reference to this verse, the Eagle). Whoever was teaching it tried to offer a new perspective on "waiting."

"Instead of 'waiting' meaning twiddling your thumbs and doing nothing," they proposed, "think of a restaurant. What do you call the person who serves your food?"

"A waiter!" answered the over-eager student in the group (it may have been me).

"Right! And if a waiter sat around and did nothing, waiting for you to finish eating, would you think they did a good job?"

"No!" The student was nailing this lesson (it was definitely me).

"Right! And so 'waiting on the Lord' really means to serve eagerly, be attentive, and stay busy while He does His work."

I can appreciate the different perspective. And we agree the Christian's responsibility to "wait on the Lord" is more active than thumb-twiddling. But this teacher made a point based on how the word wait is used in English. The original Hebrew word paints a more accurate—and frankly, more compelling—picture of waiting.

Wrapped up

The Hebrew word for "wait" in this verse is "qavah." Qavah is a rich word, originally invoking an image of a rope being twisted, wrapped, and stretched in a state of tension. You can probably feel this tension in your chest even now as you think about your current state. Like this rope, you feel pulled in two opposite directions: one, where you want to be but aren't yet, and two, where you came from but can't go back. The result of this zero-sum game of tug-of-war is feeling like you're spending all your strength, but have no progress to show for it. Waiting. It's exhausting.

But remember, qavah, "wait", is a rich Hebrew word. Keeping with the rope imagery, the Hebrew word "qavah" also carries a sense of "binding together," and offers another meaningful illustration.

Have you ever watched a well-trained dog? I don't mean a dog that only chews the old couch, I mean a dog with actual professional training. My aunt trains award-winning dogs for dog shows. Of all the tricks and commands these dogs can follow, the most impressive to us is "wait."

When the dog is told to "wait," the master can step away, walk around, and—for particularly well-trained dogs—even leave the room. Only when the master says, "Okay come!" will the dog spring into action.

If you watch the waiting dog, you'll notice how intensely focused it is. It keeps its eyes fixed on the master. If the master is out of sight, it tilts its head and perks its ears, giving its full attention until it receives the "okay." It will not move until the master says to move. And when the master says, "okay, come!" the dog is eager and ready to obey. The dog is bound to its master.

It's this understanding of "binding together" that serves us well when we find ourselves under our Master's command to "wait." Like a well-trained dog, it shouldn't matter how many distractions come up; it shouldn't matter how close or far away the reward is; it shouldn't matter if we can clearly see our Master in front of us or not. We need to bind ourselves to Him, and live in that qavah tension until He calls us to move.

New strength

In the meantime, you might feel forgotten. You might feel strung along. You might feel ignored. If so, you should know the full context of the "wings like eagles" verse:

> O Jacob, how can you say the Lord does not see your
> troubles? O Israel, how can you say God ignores your
> rights? Have you never heard? Have you never under-
> stood? The Lord is the everlasting God, the Creator of

all the earth. He never grows weak or weary. No one can measure the depths of his understanding. He gives power to the weak and strength to the powerless. Even youths will become weak and tired, and young men will fall in exhaustion. But those who trust in the Lord will find new strength. They will soar high on wings like eagles. They will run and not grow weary. They will walk and not faint. (Isaiah 40:27-31)

God makes this promise to anyone whose strength is drained as they faithfully sit in the uncomfortable tension of waiting for Him: they'll find new strength. *Waiting on God is not weakness. It's new strength.*

To continue the dog training metaphor, no one would watch a waiting dog and say, "That doesn't make any sense. It shouldn't just sit there. Why isn't it doing anything?" Because, of course, we know it's doing something quite remarkable. It's not weak or lazy. In fact, the wait demonstrates the opposite: strength, focus, and faithfulness developed over years of building the relationship. Smaller, shorter waits were requested and rewarded, and over time, they built a "waiting muscle" that can be exercised today.

Waiting on the Lord results in new strength. The longer you wait, the more strength you demonstrate, and the more strength is given when you need it. Then, when the time is right and God finally calls "okay, come!", you will take steps and not faint. Those steps will finally pick up pace to run without tiring. And, exceeding all expectations, you will fly.

Paul didn't feel like he could fly—or walk, for that matter—whenever he felt hindered by a "thorn in his flesh." He didn't specify for us what exactly the thorn was, but he felt weakened by it. Three times he begged God to remove it, but God answered,

"My grace is sufficient for you, for my power is made perfect in weakness."

"Therefore," Paul continued, "I will boast all the more gladly about my weaknesses, so that Christ's power may rest on me. That is why, for Christ's sake, I delight in weaknesses, in insults, in hardships, in persecutions, in difficulties" (1 Corinthians 12:9-10).

What follows that passage is an often-quoted piece of Scripture. Can you fill in the blanks? "For when I am weak, then ___ ___ strong."

How did you fill in those blanks? Did you say "He is"? If so, you are probably humming the tune of "Jesus Loves Me" about now. You know, "they are weak, but He is strong."

Well, believe it or not, "He is strong" is not actually the ending of Paul's sentence. The actual words are "For when I am weak, then I am strong." Really! Look it up!

Recognizing our weakness in the face of challenges and setbacks increases our strength. We are stronger for waiting.

Be still under your Banner

After the battle with the Amalekites was won, Moses set up an altar to remember God's victory. He called the altar, "Yahweh Nissi" which means, "The Lord is my Banner" (Ex. 17:15). "Yahweh Nissi"—another Name by which His people could know Him. Yahweh Nissi is the least used Name of God in Scripture. It's so infrequent, in fact, this is its only occurrence! But it's an important name to understand.

While the name itself is rare, *nissi* is a concept that shows up repeatedly. It is a banner, a flag, or a signal in battle. It's a rallying point for soldiers to gather round, a symbol that shows enemies, "as long as this banner is raised, we're not giving up."

In a Psalm commemorating a battle, King David wrote, "But you have raised a banner (*nissi*) for those who fear you—a rallying point in the face of attack" (Psalm 60:4).

God is the rallying point for you while you wait. He is held high, like the king's flag over a battle field, to remind you who you're fighting for and where your strength comes from. You can stand stronger knowing that as long as your flag is still waving, you're not giving up. And since God, Himself, is your banner, He cannot be defeated. Victory will be yours in the end because victory is already His.

How does God being your banner change the way you fight your battles?

What does rallying to Him look like?

If not to Him, what do you tend to rally to first?

In the desert of delay, while we do our part to hold steady (faithfully), God does His part to orchestrate the victory and lend us His strength. Just like Moses' friends gave him their strength, God promises to be "our refuge and strength, always ready to help in times of trouble" (Psalm 46:1).

He might not take the burden from you. He might not make the trial stop right away. But He will give you His strength while you wait. And the goal is consistent: so you will know Him and know that He is your God. You will discover what Moses learned as he held his staff, and what many of us are still learning: Yahweh Nissi uses the waiting period to let us feel weak so He can strengthen us with a different kind of strength: His. Is that enough?

Chapter Ten

The Arrival

Two months into this sojourn through the wilderness, feet aching, battle wounds still bleeding, children whining, and everyone complaining, Moses and the ragtag people of God looked across the horizon. A mountain loomed in the distance.

I imagine a sensation stirred in Moses' mind, "wait a minute... I know where we are..."

He *had* been here before. This is the stretch of wilderness where he kept his father-in-law's sheep. "That feels like a lifetime ago," he sighs.

The imposing mountain was Sinai—the same mountain where he met the God of the Hebrews in a burning bush. "You must lead my people Israel out of Egypt," the voice had said.

Moses looks around and realizes the reality of his situation. He had done it. He was at the front of this horde of people, carrying the very same staff that first turned into a snake here, wearing the same sandals he had removed on holy ground just up ahead of where he now stood. This mass of Israelites behind him now free from Egypt because he had obeyed.

A twinge of pain squinted his eyes. He didn't obey willingly. He had protested. His heart aches with the memory of that conversation.

Who am I to appear before Pharaoh? Who am I to lead the people of Israel out of Egypt? Had he really questioned the one, true God? Insinuated that Yahweh's plans were faulted? But what did God say? It's hard to recall because Moses knew his next words were still full of questions. *If I go to the people of Israel and tell them, "The God of your ancestors has sent me to you," they will ask me, "What is his name?" Then what should I tell them?*

What did God say? He looks up to the mountain, the memories rushing back, the color of the flame, the feel of the gravel under his bare feet. His eyes widen as he hears the words again, not assuring Moses of Moses' abilities, but assuring him of God's presence.

God answered, "I will be with you. And this is your sign that I am the one who has sent you: When you have brought the people out of Egypt, you will worship God at this very mountain" (Ex. 3:12).

This very mountain.

I'm back, Moses thought, blinking back tears. *The Lord said we'd all be back and worship Him here, and we are.*

Two months after leaving Egypt, Moses and the people of God arrived at the designated rendezvous point, and it was time to worship.

But this wasn't going to be a praise and worship night with a plaid-clad millennial on an acoustic guitar singing *Reckless Love.* When God Almighty planned this praise jam, He had a whole different vibe in mind.

> Then Moses climbed the mountain to appear before God. The Lord called to him from the mountain and said, "Give these instructions to the family of Jacob; announce it to the descendants of Israel: 'You have seen what I did to the Egyptians. You know how I carried you on eagles' wings and brought you to myself.

Now *if you will obey me and keep my covenant*, you will be my own special treasure from among all the peoples on earth; for all the earth belongs to me. And you will be my kingdom of priests, my holy nation.' This is the message you must give to the people of Israel." (Ex. 19:3-6 emphasis added)

To worship this God here would be to learn how to obey Him. They would learn that to know God is to obey God.

God announced He would come down the mountain and make His meeting with Moses public, in the presence of all the people. In Egypt they saw His power on display. In the desert, they had seen His heart for them come through His care, protection, healing, and deliverance. But at the mountain, they were going to see *Him*.

What was about to go down was serious, and they needed to take it seriously.

In order to prepare the people for this big move of God, and to enable them to show reverence to their holy God, they were commanded to consecrate themselves.

The summer before we got married, I (Mike) worked with Kelsey's dad to prepare their house and yard for the wedding reception in their backyard, on a lake. Let's just say my wedding prep to-do list was a lot … stinkier … than most.

I mowed the lawn, I trimmed hedges, I painted the dock, I planted flowers. I built a rock wall using big rocks that had fallen into the muck of the lake. All summer. By the end of the day, paint speckled my hair, grass clippings stained my pants, and gasoline and oil saturated my shirt. Pond scum found its way to places pond scum should never be. I reeked of the general smell of *outside*.

When the wedding day came, you better believe I showered, I rented a tuxedo, I got a fresh haircut. In doing so, I consecrated myself.

Did I have to do all that for Kelsey to love and accept me? No, and in the same way, God doesn't need you to clean up before He loves and accepts you. He loves you in your mess. And shouldn't I be generally clean all the time? Yes, and in the same way, we should always avoid sin, not just for special times.

But the main idea of consecration is *separation*. I honor Kelsey. She deserves better than me smelling like pond scum when I show up, especially on our special wedding day. I didn't work at all that day. I separated myself from all that mess, I cleaned and readied myself because she's going to stand there looking perfect, and I love her and want to honor her.

Then, anyone watching could say, "Wow, what a beautiful bride," and not, "Wow, that groom is a mess."

God asked His people to get clean, and get ready—separate from anything that doesn't represent God—to show they love and honor Him. And anyone else watching could say, "Wow, look at what happens when people follow God," and not "Wow, those people are a mess."

Cleaning up

You can read the account on your own in Exodus 19:10-15, but to summarize, there were three expectations on God's people as part of the consecration process: (1) wash their clothes, (2) abstain from sexual relations, and (3) set boundaries around the mountain they were not allowed to cross. These steps of consecration address three main areas that need our attention if we want to prepare to see God move in our lives: (1) Dirt, (2) Desires, and (3) Danger Zones.

Dirt

I (still Mike, unfortunately) spilled a bit of sauce on our area rug at home.

I retrieved our spray bottle of spot remover and treated the small stain, but I got concerned when I wiped it away, and the beige carpet around the stain turned white. Was there bleach in the bottle? It didn't say so. I grabbed another cleaning solution and tested it on another corner of the carpet. Same thing. The beige turned white. I don't think the rug got bleached; I think the rug got... clean! I rented a carpet cleaner and became morbidly enthralled as I watched the brown water spin through the powerhead and fill the tank. And you can imagine the satisfaction of restoring the rug to its original, vibrant colors.

Like an area rug in a high-traffic corridor of my house, we tend to passively collect the "dirt" and residue of daily life in this world. It rarely happens all at once; it's gradual. We brush up against the world's way of thinking as we interact with its social media, news, and movies. We match our emotions and opinions to others' emotions and opinions regarding issues facing the world. We become like those we are closest to, and sometimes those are the people at work, or the influencers we follow, or our weekend friends, who don't exactly follow Christ.

When God asked his people to wash their clothes, it represented the importance of washing away the metaphorical "dirt" of daily living. We may not even think it's gotten that bad. But compared to the bleach-white holiness of God, it doesn't take much to get dingy. The content you watch, the music you listen to, and the language and the activity of the people you associate with, can all turn your "rug" beige. Ask Him to expose the areas in your life where you have let the residue accumulate, and be ready to separate yourself from those habits or people that make you less sensitive to the heart of God.

Desires

God's command for his people to abstain from sexual relations is a surprising one for us to read, because it applied to all iterations of that activity, whether pure or impure. Obviously, God would want them to abstain from sin, but why would He want even married couples to abstain from a healthy expression of something good He created?

It's important to note here (and any time you find yourself reading about laws in the Old Testament), "unclean" does not necessarily mean "sinful". As part of the process of setting His people up to be different from the rest of the world, He declared many normal, regular activities to be unclean, after which it was necessary for them to consecrate themselves.

I'm sure it went through their heads more than once, "I can't even go a single day without being unclean!" And, well, they were right. It would have been easier to give up, surrender to the fact that life is messy, and try to not feel bad about not meeting God's expectations. But understand this: It wasn't about guilt; it was about awareness. God is holy. I am not.

God wanted to keep this awareness in the front of their mind, especially in the time before a special encounter with God. The question became, "What do you desire more? To go about your daily life unbothered? Or to have a life-changing encounter with a holy God?"

Consecration requires re-prioritizing your desires. Misplaced desires become distractions.

Even good things at the wrong time become distractions from doing the best things at the right time. When God shows up, He will expect us to respond. Will we be ready? Or will our minds be somewhere else?

Want to know the best way to identify the distractions in your life? Set a timer for 15 minutes, and either pray or read your Bible. Notice the times when your focus drifts, or your hands reach for something, or when you have an impulse to get up and do something else. There are your distractions. God will ask you to stop giving into those desires that keep you from knowing Him. Ask God to give you a heightened awareness, and strengthened resolve to prioritize the most important things.

Danger Zones

It must have been scary for the Israelites to be told that they could not approach God's mountain or step foot on it, or they would die instantly. Talk about fear of the Lord! So part of the consecration process was to agree to God's boundaries. To cross the boundary would have been to show disrespect to God.

In the case of the Israelites, the boundary was to keep them from stepping onto holy ground. Their Tabernacle had a similar boundary; only priests could cross through the curtain into the Holy Place after their own consecration process, and only the high priest could enter the second curtain into the Holy of Holies, where God's presence was recognized.

For the Israelites, the domain of their all-holy God was the danger zone. The physical boundaries of Mt. Sinai, the temple, and the law

God gave them, would serve as boundaries to keep them from accidentally stepping into it.

When Jesus died, the curtain in the temple, which served as the boundary to the Holy of Holies, was torn from top to bottom (as if God was proving He did it himself). There's no longer a boundary keeping us from approaching God. Jesus gave us access to God the Father, and we can approach God through Him.

Jesus spent much of His public teaching time redefining boundaries. Some of God's people had added so many extra laws, they became legalistic. Some had ignored so many laws, they acted the same as the pagan nations around them.

JESUS DREW BOUNDARIES KEEPING US ON HOLY GROUND, NOT AWAY FROM IT.

In both cases, their hearts were far from God. They had thought this distance from God was keeping them away from the danger zone. Jesus came to give the warning: the further you are from the heart of God, the more danger you're in.

In His first public sermon, Jesus redrew the boundary lines for God's people to observe—*not boundaries keeping us away from holy ground, but boundaries keeping us on it.*

Read these and check your heart to see if your heart has drifted away from the heart of God.

- You are the salt and light on earth. Do you give people a taste of what Jesus is like? Do you help them see Him in your life? (Matthew 5:13-14)

- Speaking and acting out of anger is as poisonous to your heart as killing someone (5:21-22).

- Do whatever it takes to stop yourself from thinking lustful thoughts. Your thought life is not safer than adultery itself

(5:27-30).

- If you mean "yes" or "no," just say so. Don't swear "on God," or on anything else for that matter. Keep your integrity intact (5:33-37).

- It's not up to you to decide what is a fair punishment for someone who hurt you. Forgive them, even if it puts you in a position where they might take advantage of you (5:38-42).

- However you show love to the people you love, show that same love to people who mistreat you (5:43-48).

- Give generously, but try to keep it between you and God (6:1-4).

- Prayer is less about the words you use, and more about the heart behind it (6:5-18).

- Worry is thinking you can control things better than God can. Instead of worrying, do God's work on earth, and try to be like Jesus (6:19-34).

"So, what?" the religious leaders challenged Jesus, "You're just going to ignore thousands of years of traditions and laws that we received from Moses himself?" Jesus clarified, "I did not come to abolish the law of Moses or the writings of the prophets. No, I came to accomplish their purpose" (Matthew 5:17).

What purpose? Paul tried to get the point across in his letter to the Galatians, who were confused by Jewish believers telling them they needed to follow the Jewish law: "Let me put it another way. The law was our guardian until Christ came; it protected us until we could be made right with God through faith. And now that the way of faith has come, we no longer need the law as our guardian" (Galatians 3:24-25).

God was, and is, as holy as ever, but He is no longer the danger zone. If you have faith in Jesus Christ, and you approach God, He doesn't see an unclean sinner. He sees His adopted child. The danger zone is anything keeping you away from this relationship. God zealously desires the danger zones to be purged from your life. The question is, are you as zealous as God when it comes to your holiness?

Holy shish-kebab

In Numbers 25, God sent a plague among his people in the wilderness, because they had intermingled with local pagan Midianites and started worshipping their god. God called for an all-in assembly, where he condemned every compromised leader to be put to death. Then the plague would be lifted.

"Just then one of the Israelite men brought a Midianite woman into his tent, right before the eyes of Moses and all the people, as everyone was weeping at the entrance of the Tabernacle" (Numbers 25:6).

This guy was so deep in the danger zone, he was completely oblivious to the gravity of the situation. But Phinehas, Aaron's grandson, wasn't going to let that foolishness go unanswered. While everyone else stared slack-jawed at the brazen act of sin, Phinehas grabbed the nearest spear, sprinted after the couple, and skewered them in the tent.

God saw a kindred spirit in Phinehas, "Phinehas son of Eleazar and grandson of Aaron the priest has turned my anger away from the Israelites by being as zealous among them as I was" (Numbers 25:11). God went on to bless Phinehas with lifelong peace with God.

Are you on the same page as God when it comes to your holiness? If you feel like we're turning up the heat: good. Like a fever helps your body kill germs that are making you sick, consecration may feel bad, but it kills the things that are making your soul sick.

Maybe you have physical things in your home that need to be thrown out. As new age philosophy ramps up in our culture, there are more and more physical items we're told are good or harmless that are inviting demonic work into your life. Those things need to be thrown out like rotten food. Books, magazines, statues, drugs, ouija boards, tarot cards, healing crystals, paraphernalia, pornography, horoscopes. These are deadly poisons. Eliminate them. Full stop. Consecrate your home. Err on the side of over-zealous. It might require throwing out things you spent money on, but it's worth your holiness. It also might mean severing relationships with the people who share those things with you. That will be difficult, but through it, you will learn another truth of who God is.

Be still and know the God who makes you holy

When you choose to no longer go to those places and partake in those activities that leave you feeling suffocated, there will be people who reject you.

When you stop pouring into relationships that cause you pain, and you stop holding space for other people's drama, and you put up healthy boundaries, there will be people who reject you.

When you repent from the sin that has been tripping you up, and you walk away and you chase after God instead, and you seek your happiness in Him and Him alone, there is a spiritual enemy who will track you down like a roaring lion and attempt to kill, steal and destroy everything good in your life.

If you're slightly overwhelmed, that's okay. If you feel too weak to give up everything and consecrate your life, that's okay. If the task of being holy seems too big, good. That's actually the point. The law was established to show people their need for a Savior. The Savior has come, and He took on the punishment for our sin. He consecrates us. It is by His power alone we are made Holy.

The law calls His people to holiness, but the Lord is the one who does the work of making us holy. *All we bring is our obedience. He provides the transformation.*

He cares about your welfare, your righteousness, and your holiness. And mostly, He wants to be with you without the dirt, desires, and danger zones in the way. So He made a way through and past those things.

"So now there is no condemnation for those who belong to Christ Jesus. And because you belong to him, the power of the life-giving Spirit has freed you from the power of sin that leads to death. So God did what the law could not do. He sent his own Son in a body like the bodies we sinners have. And in that body God declared an end to sin's control over us by giving his Son as a sacrifice for our sins." (Romans 8:1-3)

Read that again carefully. Look at the verbs used in these verses:

- The power of *the Spirit has freed you*

- *God did* what the law couldn't do

- *He sent* His own Son

- *God declared* an end to sin's control

- By *giving* his Son

The verbs belong to God. The work is done by God. All this done *for* you *by* Him, simply "because you belong to him."

It is imperative that we consecrate ourselves, that we stop looking like the world, that we prepare ourselves to be vessels ready for holy use. But we are not on our own in the process. We don't have to clean up before coming into His presence. His presence cleans us up. Ezekiel 37:27-28 depicts the end of a vision the prophet Ezekiel received regarding the reunification of the Kingdoms of Israel. God says about that time, "I will make my home among them. I will be their God, and they will be my people. And when my Temple is among them forever, the nations will know that I am the LORD, who makes Israel holy." His home being among us is what makes us holy. Because we are His, as Romans 8 says, He does this work in us and for us.

The Lord is willing to make you holy. Are you willing to stop trying, and let Him do the work?

Chapter Eleven

The Feast

Their arrival at the mountain of God was met with some strict boundaries. "Mark off a boundary all around the mountain. Warn the people, 'Be careful! Do not go up on the mountain or even touch its boundaries. Anyone who touches the mountain will certainly be put to death" (Ex. 19:12).

What followed was a thunder-and-lightning display intended to strike fear into their hearts. Then, God spoke so all the people could hear as He issued a solemn set of culture-shaping commandments (Ex. 20:1-20).

Moses climbed the mountain and received further instructions for the people. If they agreed to this new way of living, to obeying Yahweh, they would be His own special treasure.

God spoke hundreds of laws to Moses, and Moses wrote them all down.

"Then Moses went down to the people and repeated all the instructions and regulations the Lord had given him. All the people answered with one voice, 'We will do everything the Lord has commanded.' Then Moses carefully wrote down all the Lord's instructions. Then he took the Book of the Covenant and read it aloud to the people. Again they all responded, 'We will do everything the Lord has commanded. We will obey'" (Ex. 24:3-4, 7).

Obedience was, and still is, at heart of knowing God. Jesus' best friend John recognized this and penned, "And we can be sure that we know him if we obey his commandments. If someone claims, 'I know God,' but doesn't obey God's commandments, that person is a liar and is not living in the truth. But those who obey God's word truly show how completely they love him. That is how we know we are living in him. Those who say they live in God should live their lives as Jesus did" (1 John 2:3-6).

To really know God is to obey Him.

Along this journey of following God and not taking on normal jobs, we have had to come to some pretty harsh realizations. One day, as I (Kelsey) was scrolling social media mindlessly, the Lord grabbed my attention.

I stopped mid-scroll to listen to one man teach a well-known passage in Ephesians about marriage. The Holy Spirit grabbed my attention, *this is for you!*

The Lord told me to submit to my husband.

"Yeah, I know." I said out loud to either the influencer, the Holy Spirit, or both. I didn't think I *wasn't* submitting to my husband. After all, we were on the same page about this whole "living by faith" thing; we don't fight often; "and, God," I argued, "I have grown a lot more humble these past few years."

God probably rolled His eyes (He knows—and I know—I have a long way to go).

All the same, not wanting to dismiss a nudge from the Lord, I prayed into it. I asked for more understanding on how I need to submit to my husband. I don't think I need to explain to you that "submission to our husbands" is not a very modern idea of womanhood. Yet, we are called to do so regardless of culture.

In my prayer, I felt the Lord reveal to my spirit that I had been resentful at times. I had thought things like *"Why can't he just get a job and provide for our needs while we build these ministries?" "A husband should be providing, and I'm sick of not knowing where rent is coming from." "If only he hadn't left that one job… then we'd have some regular income to rely on."* I was *saying* we are on the same page, but my heart was betraying me.

The same backpack that carries resentment also carries a desire for control. As long as I held onto resentment, I also held a desire to control my situation and my outcomes. A desire to control where my family was headed meant I also wanted to control what God was doing in our lives.

When I got very honest with myself and God, I realized that I wasn't fully on board with where and how Mike was leading us. I didn't fully trust him. And since he was following God's lead, I wasn't trusting God. My lack of submission to my husband actually meant a lack of submission to my God.

My actions were following along, but my heart was fighting against this plan that made me very uncomfortable and required constant relinquishing of my will. God isn't here to make us comfortable. Wishing for my own comfort in life when He was leading my husband in a different direction meant I wasn't only disobeying God, I was fighting Him.

I'm guessing, since you're reading this book, you have a desire to know God. I also believe you want to obey Him. It's hard, though, isn't it? It feels like despite our best intentions, despite how much we desire God, despite how much of the Bible we read, there's a stubborn part of us that bucks at the very concept of obedience.

The painful truth is that in order for us to live in obedience, something else has to die.

To know God is to obey God. And to obey God is to make sacrifices.

The cost of sacrifice

Imagine a pasture with dozens of sheep. They're your sheep. Each sheep represents something valuable to you. Some may be tangible things: your home, your car, your phone. Others are intangible: your job, your insurance, your health. Some are concepts like your plans, your goals, your comfort. While others are relational: your spouse, your children, your friends. See them prancing around your life-pasture together? Look at them all. So cute.

Now, if God walks up to your pasture with a butcher's knife, what sheep are you running to first, to scoop up and protect from God?

Your answers reveal the areas where it will be hardest to obey God.

Of course, I'm not saying God is out to get you and kill everything and everyone you love. But obedience will require the death of something that has some value to you. The value He offers in exchange—knowing Him more deeply—is worth it in His eyes. Is it worth it in yours?

Following the Lord's instructions, Moses sacrificed some animals. He took the blood on the altar and from the basins, and declared, "Look, this blood confirms the covenant the Lord has made with you in giving you these instructions" (Ex. 24:8).

The people blinked and winced in surprise and disgust as Moses proceeded to dip his fingers in the blood and splatter them with it.

Gross? Yes. Sacrifice is messy. Covenants are not cheap. The Israelites watched the life drain from the faces of innocent animals, and suppressed their gags as the warm, wet blood dripped down their faces. This covenant with God was not for their comfort or convenience. It was a blood covenant, sealed with the blood of an animal killed on their behalf. The blood was poured out in obedience, and demanded a response of obedience itself, or else the animal's life would have been given in vain.

If this sounds familiar, good. That's the point. Every sacrifice of every animal under the Mosaic covenant was pointing toward the Lamb of God who would be led to slaughter, murdered publicly, and held up in front of the people. Warm, wet sacrificial blood dripped down on those who mourned Him, and would cover all who would ever call on the name of Jesus to be saved. This sacrifice would be once and for all people, for all of time.

Fortunately, today, we are no longer under the Mosaic covenant. We live under the new covenant between God and men—the covenant of Jesus Christ that says it is by faith that we are saved through faith, and not by works so that no man can boast (Ephesians 2:8-9).

TO KNOW GOD IS TO OBEY GOD. TO OBEY GOD IS TO MAKE SACRIFICES.

But this new covenant does not mean there aren't some expectations on how we live. Free grace does not give us freedom to live however we want (Romans 6:1-2). When we accept Jesus' sacrifice on our behalf, we also die to ourselves (Galatians 2:20). Our desires, our plans, all must be submitted to Him. That's what makes Him our Lord.

To know God is to obey God. To obey God is to make sacrifices. But our sacrifices are only a response to God's ultimate sacrifice.

A tale of two mountains

After the reading of the covenant, the blood shower, and the people's agreement to obey, God invited the leaders of Israel—Moses, Aaron, Nadab, Abihu, and seventy elders—to come up to the mountain.

You might remember, God said He'd kill anyone who even touched the mountain. An animal that crossed the boundary must be shot with an arrow, and anyone who tried to help it must be stoned. Moses, remembered, too. But God was extending an opportunity for His people to know Him. God doesn't make covenants from a distance.

> Then Moses, Aaron, Nadab, Abihu, and the seventy elders of Israel climbed up the mountain. There they saw the God of Israel. Under his feet there seemed to be a surface of brilliant blue lapis lazuli, as clear as the sky itself. And though these nobles of Israel gazed upon God, he did not destroy them. *In fact, they ate a covenant meal, eating and drinking in his presence.* (Ex. 24:9-11, emphasis added)

Isn't this amazing? After the lightning, the thunder, and the restrictions. After the sacrifice, the blood, and the obedience. God initiated an opportunity to know Him in a way that makes a lot of sense to us food-motivated humans: He shared a meal.

We believe the elders in this story ate this covenant meal with Jesus Himself. After all, this would not be the only meal Jesus eats and drinks with His beloved people to confirm covenants.

The night Jesus was betrayed, before being handed over to authorities who would wrongly accuse him and sentence him to death, He instituted the *new* covenant through His blood. "This cup is the new covenant between God and his people—an agreement confirmed with my blood, which is poured out as a sacrifice for you" (Luke 22:20).

This meal and new covenant were shared in the mountain-top capital city of Jerusalem, or, as it's sometimes called, Zion. God's Word uses this as a metaphor and offers you another invitation:

> You have not come to a physical mountain, to a place of flaming fire, darkness, gloom, and whirlwind, as the Israelites did at Mount Sinai. For they heard an awesome trumpet blast and a voice so terrible that they begged God to stop speaking. They staggered back under God's command: "If even an animal touches the mountain, it must be stoned to death." Moses himself was so frightened at the sight that he said, "I am terrified and trembling." (Hebrews 12:18-21)

Pause. This book is titled *The Mountain in the Desert*. We've talked a lot about your desert, what it represents, and how to navigate this season. But what about the mountain? What do you think about when you think of God? Does God seem unsafe to you? Maybe He has seemed destructive like fire. Obscure, like darkness. Heartbreaking, like gloom. Unpredictable, like a whirlwind. Maybe you've begged God to stop speaking, and staggered back from what seemed unfair. Maybe you've heard the term "the fear of God," and what comes to mind is the fear of an oppressive, cold, volatile father.

The thought of obeying such a God would mean either obeying out of obligation and fear of consequences, or not obeying at all, out of rebellion.

If this resonates with you, I hope you're beginning to see this is not the God who is inviting you to know Him more. The metaphor continues,

> No, you have come to Mount Zion, to the city of the living God, the heavenly Jerusalem, and to countless thousands of angels in a joyful gathering. You have come to the assembly of God's firstborn children, whose names are written in heaven. You have come to God himself, who is the judge over all things. You have come to the spirits of the righteous ones in heaven who have now been made perfect. You have come to Jesus, the one who mediates the new covenant between God and people, and to the sprinkled blood, which speaks of forgiveness instead of crying out for vengeance like the blood of Abel. (Hebrews 12:22-24)

Pause again. Maybe your heart sings at this description. This is the gospel, and it's beautiful. How blessed are we to come to the throne, to come to Jesus and receive God's covenant with gratitude and praise. Forgiveness, not guilt, characterizes your relationship with God.

But surely, an understanding of God's forgiveness opens the door to withholding our sacrifice of obedience, and abusing how much grace He's willing to offer.

Be still and approach

It's here we come across another tension of Christian living: the tension between fearing the Lord and approaching the Lord. How can we approach God like His beloved children, but also maintain a healthy reverence for the King of Kings? How can we live in sacrificial obedience and feel neither coldly obligated nor loosely non-committal? The writer of Hebrews goes on to issue a warning and a direction:

> Be careful that you do not refuse to listen to the One who is speaking. For if the people of Israel did not escape when they refused to listen to Moses, the earthly messenger, we will certainly not escape if we reject the One who speaks to us from heaven! When God spoke from Mount Sinai his voice shook the earth, but now he makes another promise: "Once again I will shake not only the earth but the heavens also." This means that all of creation will be shaken and removed, so that only unshakable things will remain.
> Since we are receiving a Kingdom that is unshakable, let us be thankful and please God by worshiping him with holy fear and awe. For our God is a devouring fire. (Hebrews 12:25-29)

Mount Sinai was surrounded by a boundary to keep Israel safe. But through Christ, we come to Mount Zion, where we are welcomed to approach God. How?

1. With gratitude. Gratitude carries the tension of joy for what

God has done, with the humility that we don't deserve it.

2. With worship. Worship puts God in His proper place, high above us, yet among the assembly of His children.

3. With holy fear. Fear, not like we're afraid of God, but afraid of hurting our relationship by our sin.

4. With awe. Awe, because a devouring fire is pleasant when it consumes our obedient sacrifices, and painful when disrespected.

With this posture, approach God to feast in the intimacy He offers. He chooses to be at peace with us, even when we have given Him every reason not to be.

Chapter Twelve

The Cloud

Like a teacher who asks a student to stay behind while the rest of the class is dismissed, God summoned Moses and Joshua to stay and talk after the feast. The other leaders could return to camp. God put Aaron in charge in case any issues came up.

For forty days and forty nights, Moses was hidden with God inside a massive cloud that settled on the mountain. But of course, the rest of the people of Israel didn't know it would be forty days and forty nights. A few days went by. "He must be hungry up there. Or maybe there's food on the mountain we don't know about?" Days turned into a week. "Has anyone seen Moses? Is he still up there?" Weeks turned into a month. "Maybe he died. Did God kill him? Maybe God took him away like Enoch. Who's in charge now? Aaron! Find Aaron! He'll know what to do!" By the time day forty rolled around, Aaron himself wasn't sure what to think.

Sometimes, when it feels like God isn't speaking or moving, all you see is a cloud. A foggy curtain draped over your soul. It's easy to feel like God is taking too long. Like the Israelites, you might feel abandoned. Is God even with me anymore?

Before we move on with the story, let's sit with this question:

"Is the cloudy presence of God enough?"

Mike and I have wrestled with this question in many areas of life, not the least of which is finances. There's a phrase that keeps coming to my mind when I am sitting with our budget, when we get an inquiry for a gig, or when I'm praying for provision. In those moments, I tend to think, "If we can hit this financial goal ... If this gig will just come through before the end of the month ... If we could just see God do this ... *then I won't have to worry.*"

It's that last part of the phrase that stops me in my tracks lately. "... then I won't have to worry."

I hear the Holy Spirit gently whisper, "Why do you *have* to worry at all?"

Like Moses recalls in Deuteronomy 29:5-6, "For forty years I led you through the wilderness, yet your clothes and sandals did not wear out. You ate no bread and drank no wine or other alcoholic drink, but he provided for you so you would know that he is the Lord your God."

They weren't living extravagantly with wine and bread. But they were provided for, and their shoes didn't wear out. That was miraculous! We've wondered if God's provision for us is like that. We aren't living the high life, but our car hasn't broken down, and our clothes don't have holes.

It can feel like a cloudy presence of God, though. He's not lavishly pouring out His favor, but He is keeping us housed. We aren't seeing excessive provision, but we aren't in financial deficit. Is that God? I look up to heaven and cry out sometimes, "God! Is that you? This minor miracle that our kid's shoes fit for a whole school year—is that you?" I'll be honest, it would feel better if we simply had enough money to buy new shoes. But what about when the shoes just don't wear out? Is the cloudy provision of God enough?

What provision are we overlooking? Will we only recognize God's hand in something when it's big and flashy? When the thunder rolls and the lightning strikes? Are we holding back our worship for when He brings us out of the desert and we can look back and see His hand clearly? Can we recognize His care for us in the steady, faithful, and unremarkable days? And if those are the only days we get, is that enough?

It's during God's cloudy presence that it's easiest to turn around and look for an exit strategy. When we don't know what God's doing, where He is, or what He's saying, we can tend to respond like the Israelites did.

Tribal leaders cornered Aaron to voice the opinion of the people. There had been no sign of Moses for almost six weeks—he was dead for all they knew—and they were getting anxious. "It's dangerous here in the wilderness, man! Without some god to protect us, we're not gonna make it! Give us someone to worship!"

I don't know if it was peer pressure or heat stroke, but Aaron agreed! An idea came to mind.

He instructed the people to gather their gold to melt it down.

How much gold could a desert-wandering group of ex-slaves have for this project? Quite a bit, it turns out. When the Israelites were finally released from Egypt, the locals—freshly reeling from the deaths of their firstborn—showered them with "good riddance" gifts:

> All the Egyptians urged the people of Israel to get out
> of the land as quickly as possible, for they thought,
> "We will all die!" ... And the people of Israel did as

Moses had instructed; they asked the Egyptians for clothing and articles of silver and gold. The Lord caused the Egyptians to look favorably on the Israelites, and they gave the Israelites whatever they asked for. So they stripped the Egyptians of their wealth! (Ex. 12:33, 35-36)

Did you catch the fact that this was the Lord's way to provide for His people? Wild, crazy provision. Gold, silver, clothing. More than they would need. God set them up to rebuild their lives, to survive and thrive in the promised land. God had provided for them.

And now, out of fear, they took that provision, melted it down, and formed a golden god in the shape of a calf. But it gets worse.

"When the people saw it, they exclaimed, "O Israel, these are the gods who brought you out of the land of Egypt!" (Ex. 32:4).

The people took their God-given provision, idolized it as something they could see and understand, and then credited that idol with their freedom and security.

They credited the provision God gave them as if it saved them. They praised the provision instead of the Provider. They worshipped the means instead of the Waymaker.

THEY CREDITED THE PROVISION GOD GAVE THEM AS IF IT SAVED THEM.

God was sick with anger. "I have seen how stubborn and rebellious these people are. Now leave me alone so my fierce anger can blaze against them, and I will destroy them" (Ex. 32:9-10). They knew better! Mere weeks ago, Aaron and seventy leaders shared a meal at His table!

Idolatry is a slap to God's face. An idol is anything we go to in hopes of receiving what we can only truly receive from God: peace, protection, health, provision.

You may not be laying everything down at the feet of a golden cow, but are you checking your bank account to make sure you have enough to take care of you in an emergency?

Is a peaceful sleep so elusive that your pint, puff, or pill is within arms' reach of your bed?

Are you so concerned with what may or may not be happening in the world, that the first thing you read or watch in the morning is the news?

Are you so afraid of feeling alone that you'll spend the night with any guy or girl or video that makes you feel something?

Do you consider your spouse—and I'm aware how prickly this is—to be your "rock", so much so that you have no idea what you would do without them?

Here's a hard truth: *As long as you are relying on anything other than God to get you out of the wilderness, God is not interested in getting you out of the wilderness.*

The most common idol in our modern day is not much different than the golden calf in the desert. We tend to worship money. We only have it because God has allowed us to receive it. When we need something, money can provide it. Then we wipe our brow, relieved that our emergency fund was enough to cover the unexpected expenses.

Mike and I have done it, and we know you have, too. We don't make paper-mâché with our Benjamins and bow down in front of an arts and crafts project. But we do tend to think:

"We'll be okay if we have enough money in the savings account."

"I'll feel secure if we have a retirement plan."

"If I take this job and work this many hours, I'll make enough money that I won't have to worry." As if without the money we *have* to worry.

Jesus put it this way, in Matthew 6:24, "No one can serve two masters. For you will hate one and love the other; you will be devoted to one and despise the other. You cannot serve God and be enslaved to money."

You can't trust money for your security and trust God at the same time. It's not possible. We cannot rely on God's promises for tomorrow *and* rely on our financial situation to give us peace for the future.

Being enslaved to money can look like:

- working more hours to afford the life we want.

- fighting for a better position at work to give us the raise and respect we think we deserve.

- neglecting God's instruction to give generously because we don't think we'll have enough left to buy what we need

- worrying about our house, our clothes, and our food

Jesus understands your predicament, and wants better for you. "These things dominate the thoughts of unbelievers, but your heavenly Father already knows all your needs," He says in Matthew 6:32. Jesus repeats the phrase, "Do not worry." Quite simply, when Jesus says to not do something, and we do it, that is sin.

Anything dominating our thoughts is an idol. And it is sin.

Let us clarify: you aren't necessarily in this wilderness of delay *because* of your sin or your idols. The wait is not necessarily a punishment. But when God is cloudy, we tend to look elsewhere for the way out, and that is when we tend to turn to idols. At that point, God may prolong your pause to give you an opportunity to recognize, and then deal with, your sin. The way forward will not likely show itself until the idols are crushed and our hearts repent.

Furthermore, we're not suggesting *repentance* is a magical ticket out of the wilderness. You might repent and God *still* has more for you in the delay. But we can be confident that without repentance, there is no hope of leaving this wilderness season behind.

I (Mike) could have never imagined the impact of the 2020 pandemic on my family's finances. It was like someone turned off the faucet and tightened it with a wrench. My income was slashed completely. Kelsey's already-meager church staff salary was cut another twenty percent.

We tried as long as we could to hold onto God's promise to provide all we needed if we would stay faithful to seeking the Kingdom first. But God was silent for a long time. The mountain was extremely cloudy. Without a clear way forward, and genuinely not knowing where our help was coming from, I looked at our bank account and felt the desperation of our situation. I have always been the one responsible for giving God a tenth back of whatever comes in, but I had never experienced so little coming in. So I stopped tithing. Every trickling dollar felt precious and there was never enough of it. By my calculations, we couldn't afford to give any of it away.

That year, not coincidentally, was also the year we went into debt for the first time in our marriage. We watched in misery as dollars, dreams, and joy drained from our days. And God let us stay miserable for a long while.

Until we came to our knees to repent.

We had to repent for our hoarding what we had. But more than the dollars we didn't give, we had to repent for abandoning trust. We chose to cling to the provision instead of the Provider. We thought more money would get us out of our desert; we were wrong. We desperately needed to repent. And then, *only then*, did God begin to slowly turn our financial situation around.

Be still and know the jealousy of God

When Israel formed and worshipped the golden calf, it put a relational rift between God and His people. He was furious and threatened to destroy them all. Fascinatingly, Moses was allowed to intercede. "The Lord changed his mind about the terrible disaster he had threatened to bring on his people" (Ex. 32:14).

But in the conversation that followed, God offered Moses and Israel a wild deal. Everything you want: The Promised Land for you and your descendants, an angel to wipe out your enemies, safety, and prosperity. Just one condition: "I will not travel among you, for you are a stubborn and rebellious people. If I did, I would surely destroy you along the way" (Ex. 33:3).

I'll be honest with you. I'd be tempted to take that deal. I could have what I've been dreaming about for years, and the struggle to get there could be over? All my needs could be met, and difficult people would leave me alone? Come on, that sounds better and better as I write it. I can't be the only one who would at least consider it.

God presented two options to move forward. It blows my mind to learn that Moses recognized and begged for a third option. "If you don't personally go with us, don't make us leave this place" (Ex. 33:15).

What faith! What a relationship! God, if we wouldn't even survive the trip with you—and I believe you're right—and if completing the trip means being without you ... then *we'd rather stay here in the desert—with you—for the rest of our lives!*

Can you say the same? Think of the desert season you're languishing in today. Are you willing to live like this for the rest of your life if it was the only way you could be with God?

It's okay if the answer isn't "yes" right now. And God's not mad at you if you're not in the same place Moses was. This attitude toward God is forged in the desert and tempered on the mountain. It's the fruit God had been cultivating in Moses this entire journey, and is fostering in you, with time. Moses put words to the truth we need to discover in our own deserts: "Your presence among us sets your people and me apart from all other people on the earth" (Ex. 33:16b).

Don't let that truth get lost in this chapter. God's presence in your life is what sets you apart from everyone who does not follow Him. And without it, you have nothing worth living for.

With this greater understanding of God's heart, Yahweh invited Moses even closer. He granted Moses' request, and then allowed Moses to witness a glimpse of His glory:

> Then the Lord came down in a cloud and stood there with him; and he called out his own name, Yahweh. The Lord passed in front of Moses, calling out, "Yahweh! The Lord! The God of compassion and mercy! I am slow to anger and filled with unfailing love and faithfulness. I lavish unfailing love to a thousand generations. I forgive iniquity, rebellion, and sin. But I do

not excuse the guilty. I lay the sins of the parents upon their children and grandchildren; the entire family is affected—even children in the third and fourth generations." Moses immediately threw himself to the ground and worshiped. (Ex. 34:5-8)

Have you ever heard someone claim that the God of the Old Testament is wrathful, but the God of the New Testament is Love? That is a lie from the liar. God doesn't change, and the heart of God that Moses learned, we can discover today. His declaration of Himself in this passage shows He is the God of compassion and mercy! He is slow to anger and filled with unfailing love and faithfulness. That sounds like it could be a quote out of Jesus' mouth in the book of John, but it's right here, in the midst of God allowing Moses to change His mind to not destroy the adulterous people of Israel.

But they were adulterous, idolatrous, and that behavior was unacceptable within this relationship.

A few verses later, God says to Moses, "You must worship no other gods, for the Lord, whose very name is Jealous, is a God who is jealous about his relationship with you" (Ex. 34:14).

The word *jealous* is almost always used as a negative emotion today. The fact that God describes Himself as *Jealous* has caused many to misunderstand and dismiss God as petty and insecure. But if I (Kelsey) think about the relationships that mean the most to me, *jealous* doesn't sound insecure. My husband *should* be jealous for me if he loves me. What would it say of his character and our relationship if He was okay with me sleeping around and flirting with other guys? And, of course, because I love him, I avoid doing things that stir up jealousy in him. Our relationship is stronger if I only have eyes for him, and he for me.

The same is true for God. He does not want to share you with people, ideologies, and sins that have no regard for you and your relationship with Him. He is jealous about His relationship with you. And this name, Jealous, is unique in that it is one He gives Himself. Many other names were discovered and spoken by people building an altar or recognizing God in a new way. But God says of Himself, "the Lord, whose very name is Jealous, is a God who is jealous about his relationship with you."

Going to anything else other than God for the things you need is committing adultery in your relationship with Him. Idolatry is adultery. God will not share you with another god. God will not share your worship, your trust, your praise, your adoration. And I find that comforting.

If you only knew ...

I believe the reason God was so angry about the golden calf was because they were inviting another god into the intimacy He was preparing to share with them.

Ultimately, the Israelites wanted a god they could encamp with. They wanted a god to be in their presence to give them security and comfort. They wanted the god they worshipped to be *with* them. That's the saddest thing about this part of the story.

What were Moses and Yahweh doing on that mountain for those forty days and forty nights? While the people below were impatiently replacing God with an image they could interact with, Moses was downloading from God the blueprints for what the people wanted most: a way to commune with God. For forty days and forty nights, God was giving Moses the beautiful picture of what it would look like when God came down from the mountain to dwell with His people. God wanted to be with them even more than they could imagine.

Paul wrote about their time in the wilderness:

> I don't want you to forget, dear brothers and sisters, about our ancestors in the wilderness long ago. All of them were guided by a cloud that moved ahead of them, and all of them walked through the sea on dry ground. In the cloud and in the sea, all of them were baptized as followers of Moses. All of them ate the same spiritual food, and all of them drank the same spiritual water. For they drank from the spiritual rock that traveled with them, and that rock was Christ. Yet God was not pleased with most of them, and their bodies were scattered in the wilderness. These things happened as a warning to us, so that we would not crave evil things as they did. (1 Corinthians 10:1-6)

What you crave is what you will worship. The Israelites craved something other than Yahweh, so they worshipped something other than Him. Their end is a warning to us. Let us crave Jesus. Let us worship only Him. Let us turn only to Him for all of our needs.

Chapter Thirteen

The Gift

God had one thing to say on repeat throughout much of the Old Testament and certainly throughout Exodus: "So that they will know I am their God." The miracles, the milestones, the victories, the punishments, all were intended to show His people who He is so they would know He is their God.

His desire was to be theirs and for them to be His. Like a bride and a groom claiming possession over one another in love, God claimed His people and wanted them to claim Him. And much like a newlywed couple, He wanted a dwelling place, a home in which this relationship could grow and thrive. His plan was a Tabernacle. "Tabernacle" is a word that means "dwell among." He had brought the Hebrews out of slavery, provided through starvation, awarded victory in battles, and established a law to set them apart. All of it was showing His people who He is so He could establish a relationship with them. The Tabernacle was the final phase of His plans during the Exodus. The Tabernacle would be how He established His presence with His people.

And it was glorious.

The people contributed generously to the project, probably a bit motivated to make up for the whole "golden calf" incident. God called out the most skilled craftsmen to oversee the work. This was the most important work they had undertaken in their lives! These artisans were finally building for God instead of for slave drivers. Finally using their skills to worship Yahweh instead of aggrandizing Pharaoh. There was a lot to get done, and once the people offered their valuable materials for the construction, there was nothing stopping them from getting to work.

Except God. He had another stop for His people before work began.

I (Kelsey) have a bad habit. When I'm working on a project, whether it's making a big dinner, decorating for a party, or producing a stage production, I all-too-often get into "work mode" at the expense of people. Here's what I mean: Mike and I were preparing to present an Outloud Bible Experience to our home church the week of Easter. He prepared to read the second half of the book of John in his unique, dramatized way. And I had spent days planning the musical underscoring and lighting design. The night before the performance, I couldn't sleep because of my excitement and ideas.

The next day, we rolled into the church to set up. My brother offered to help run the lighting, so he met us there. I think the first words I said to him were, "do we have the ability to have a spotlight or is it only a wash of the whole stage?" I'm admitting here on paper, to my shame, I don't think I even said "hi." I was so excited about the work—good work, God glorifying ministry work—but I forgot to spend time with the people.

God knows this about us. He knows that when we get a project, an idea, a directive, we can all get into "work mode" and kind of forget the things that matter most. Even when the work is ordained by God Himself, there is something more important than the work: Him.

Before God gave instructions for building His Tabernacle, He gave a reminder. Before the whistle blew for the start of the work day, He gave a command to rest.

> Then Moses called together the whole community of Israel and told them, "These are the instructions the Lord has commanded you to follow. You have six days each week for your ordinary work, but the seventh day must be a Sabbath day of complete rest, a holy day dedicated to the Lord. Anyone who works on that day must be put to death. (Ex. 35:1-2)

God had given Moses Ten Commandments amidst a covenant of about 613 laws. Yet before breaking ground on the most important project of His people's life, God gave an inaugural address in which He repeated only one of those laws: Sabbath.

Sabbath was given within the first iteration of the Ten Commandments:

> Remember to observe the Sabbath day by keeping it holy. You have six days each week for your ordinary work, but the seventh day is a Sabbath day of rest dedicated to the Lord your God. On that day no one in

your household may do any work. This includes you, your sons and daughters, your male and female servants, your livestock, and any foreigners living among you. (Ex. 20:8-10)

It was later reiterated as part of the terms for God to be with His people going forward after their rebellion: "You have six days each week for your ordinary work, but on the seventh day you must stop working, even during the seasons of plowing and harvest" (Ex. 34:21).

Because Sabbath is a part of the Mosaic Law, some Christians today will say it is no longer for us, because we are no longer under the law. But Sabbath, while part of the law, was established before the law. God demonstrated Sabbath rest at creation as an example for His people for all time. "For in six days the Lord made the heavens, the earth, the sea, and everything in them; but on the seventh day he rested. That is why the Lord blessed the Sabbath day and set it apart as holy" (Ex. 20:11). If God did it as an example to us, we ought to take it seriously.

God ordained a Sabbath rest for His people even before giving the law with the example of creation. He instituted Sabbath back when they were picking up manna in the wilderness. His heart behind the Sabbath is shared: "They must realize that the Sabbath is the Lord's gift to you" (Ex. 16:29).

Now, if we're debating "what in the Old Testament do I have to obey and what doesn't apply any more?" we're missing the point. The question ought to be "what is God's heart, and how do I align myself with Him?"

Do you see one full day of rest every week as a gift? Or is a full day of rest in the way of progress?

Some people will argue, "I really need to complete this project. If I try to rest, I'll be thinking about it anyway, so I'll just keep working to get it done." Others may be motivated by provision: the more hours you work, the more money you make. Some are motivated by prestige, the people in charge at your company think highly of hard work and they reward those who prove dedicated to the cause. Still others don't think they've *earned* rest, so they keep working while they await the non-existent sign they've earned some downtime.

If God commanded His people to rest on the seventh day *even while building His home*, how much more ought you to rest from your earthly work? Psalm 127 makes it very clear that any work done under our own power is done in vain.

> Unless the Lord builds a house, the work of the builders is wasted. Unless the Lord protects a city, guarding it with sentries will do no good. It is useless for you to work so hard from early morning until late at night, anxiously working for food to eat; for God gives rest to his loved ones. (Psalm 127:1-2)

Working seven days a week doesn't necessarily mean you're at the office seven days a week, or pulling a paycheck 24/7. Saturdays can be filled with errands you didn't accomplish during the week and extracurricular activities for the kids. This kind of Saturday is not Sabbath. Sunday may be a day for church, shopping, and planning for the week ahead. This kind of Sunday is not Sabbath.

When God established Sabbath, it included working hard enough during the week that the seventh day's responsibilities were covered. If your to-do list on the weekend is just as full as your to-do list during the week, you are not taking a Sabbath. Just because the activities are different does not mean they're restful.

The importance of Sabbath cannot be understated.

I would suggest that the part of Sabbath law that no longer applies under the new covenant is the punishment of death for breaking Sabbath. If you work all weekend, no one will slaughter you and your family. But the reality that death was the punishment under the Mosaic Law ought to lend weight to its importance in God's eyes. To ignore God's heart for rest is to think your way is better than His.

The root of overwork is pride. Refusing to rest is declaring you can accomplish more in seven days than God can in six. Time is given to us by God, just like money. Earlier, we explored how letting go of money is an act of trust. In the same way tithing demonstrates trust that God will meet our needs even without 1/10 of our income, a Sabbath rest places our trust that God will help us accomplish the work even without 1/7 of our week. Otherwise, you're placing your trust in your own abilities, planning, and energy.

It's the rhythm that's important. Sabbath is a weekly rhythm of submission to the Lord. No matter how much I get lost in my own efforts and my own problems during the week, a weekly Sabbath serves to anchor me to who is really in charge. "Tell the people of Israel: 'Be careful to keep my Sabbath day, for the Sabbath is a sign of the covenant between me and you from generation to generation. It is given so you may know that I am the Lord, who makes you holy'" (Ex. 31:13). The Sabbath reminds us that it is the Lord who makes us holy. Not our works, not our efforts. Whatever I do during the week, in whatever way I fail or succeed, Sabbath reminds me that the covenant is based on Jesus' sacrifice and it is not my effort that keeps me in covenant with Him; the Lord makes me holy. He is the Lord and I am not.

Be still and know the God who rests

God's presence is established God's way. The fact that the Tabernacle construction was not begun until a Sabbath was observed suggests rest is a necessary rhythm to experiencing God's presence in our lives.

I (Kelsey) recently had a conversation with a very close friend where we were talking about the dangers of overwork and his lack of rest. He works full time and he's also very involved in ministry at church and music ministry on the weekends. I said something along the lines of "what if Jesus doesn't want you to *do* anything? What if all the good things you think you're doing with your time isn't what He wants from you?" He asked, "Is there no room in there for using my skills, talents, and experience?"

The way things unfold in Exodus 35-40 provides an excellent answer to that question. Women used their skills in creating the fabric for the Tabernacle: "All the women who were skilled in sewing and spinning prepared blue, purple, and scarlet thread, and fine linen cloth" (Ex. 35:25). Men were assigned leadership in the construction based on their skills and experience, "The Lord has filled Bezalel with the Spirit of God, giving him great wisdom, ability, and expertise in all kinds of crafts (Ex. 35:31)."

There was clearly room for their skills and experience. But those things came into play *after* God commanded them to honor the Sabbath.

GOD DOES NOT INVITE YOUR SKILLS AT THE EXPENSE OF REST.

You may be highly skilled in your job. You may have talents that the church needs in order to grow and serve your community. You can possess valuable experience that God wants to use to bring His Kingdom to earth. But *God does not invite your skills at the expense of rest.*

Sabbath has been one of the sweetest gifts to our family over the past several years. In this long season of not having jobs, searching for purpose, and waiting on God's plans, Sabbath has become an anchor of rest for our souls. Depending on the week, it might be Saturday. It might be Monday. But a week doesn't go by without one. These intentional days of rest have trained our family to be more present with each other. We are able to enjoy one another's company without doing anything specific. We are less rushed and panicked during the week. If it didn't get done by Sabbath, it'll get done next week. There's no use worrying about tomorrow; it'll worry about itself. When we Sabbath, we are being trained to let worries go.

What would it take for you to do less on your days off? Would you consider being still so you can rest and know that He is God? It might require saying "no" to some people and their plans. It might mean you have extra chores earlier in the week. But it will also mean your relationship with God is deepened. Your family will grow closer as you learn how to simply *be* without having to *do* anything. Your worries will lessen when the rhythm of Sabbath continually reminds you who is really in charge.

May we be people who rest, who trust God enough to honor the Sabbath. Literally, for the love of God, stop.

Chapter Fourteen

The Tent

With Sabbath established, it was time to begin the construction of the Tabernacle. Men and women eagerly donated all the materials for the tent and furnishings. Two skilled craftsmen were named to take charge of the project: Bezelel and Oholiab. The Holy Spirit empowered them with every skill needed to fashion the dwelling place for the Most High to live among His people.

But the Tabernacle was more than the fanciest tent on the block. It was greater than the sum of its wool, gold, onyx stones, and acacia wood.

A hint of the real thing

In the spring of our daughter's Kindergarten year, her class painted little pots, filled them with soil, planted little seeds in that soil, and learned about how plants grow over the next few weeks. Children were filled with awe as their seedlings sprouted up from the soil. Their little watering cans were like magic wands, helping something new appear where there was once only dirt. The teacher took care to time this botany lesson so that each small pot would be host to a colorful flower in time for Mother's Day.

Our sweet girl was aglow with pride as she handed me (Kelsey) her carefully curated blossom.

Unbeknownst to her, she has a mother who can't keep plants alive. The flower died in two days.

Now, I sit at a desk adorned with LEGO™ flowers. I have nine plastic pots and nine shiny petaled reflections of nature. They aren't the real thing, because I can't handle the real thing. But they remind me of the beauty of God's creation outside.

The Tabernacle was like this. The writer of Hebrews tells us that the Tabernacle described in Exodus was a copy of the throne room in heaven (Hebrews 8:5). We can't handle the real thing, so God gave His people a LEGO™ set of what heaven looks like! How cool is it that when we look at the Tabernacle, we can catch a reminder of the beauty of heaven where Christ now sits!

For the Hebrews in the desert, the Tabernacle was a physical representation of God's presence among them. And God took great care in describing each element of its construction. God gave instruction to Moses to recreate His heavenly throne room in human-made furnishings to give us a glimpse of His glory; to remind us who sits on the throne of the universe. The Tabernacle was in the center of their camp reminding them to keep God at the center of their lives.

Today, the physical Tabernacle has come and gone, replaced by temples which were eventually torn down by invading kingdoms. But because it represented our lasting home, heaven, its message is no less important for us today.

Would you join me on a brief tour of the Tabernacle and learn more about the heart of God along the way?

THE TABERNACLE

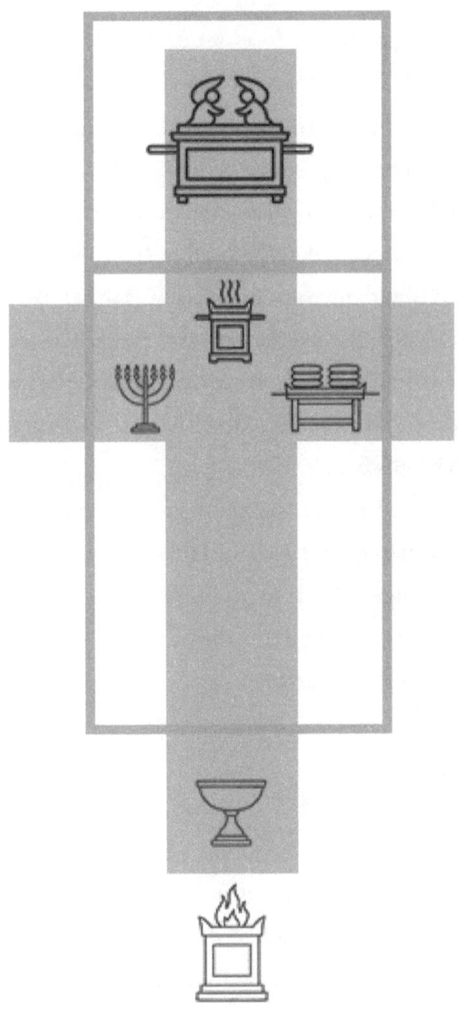

the cross-shaped design of the Tabernacle

Foretelling furniture

Under God's instruction, Moses set up the six pieces of furniture of the Tabernacle in the shape of a cross (Ex. 40). This connection to Jesus' death is not overtly mentioned, but the layout is precisely described. We have the privilege of looking back with hindsight of the cross of Christ and recognizing the the beautiful metaphor of the Tabernacle. One piece was at the head of the cross, one stood where the two beams would intersect, one piece at each hand, one at the place where the feet would be, and the sixth at the base. The care with which God the Father told the story of redemption for His people displays His heart for you and for me. His desire has always been to be our God, and for us to be His people.

The Tabernacle had an outer court, an inner court called the Holy Place, and a set apart room called the Holy of Holies—the place where God's very presence resided. As you walk from outside of the Tabernacle through the rooms and past the furniture, you are brought into closer intimacy with the Father.

Altar of Sacrifice

The first thing people would encounter when they entered the outer court of the Tabernacle was the Altar of Sacrifice. The parallel was made very clear by John the Baptist when he said of Jesus, "behold the lamb of God who takes away the sins of the world!" (John 1:29) The Jewish law of sacrificing an animal to take away the sin of one person, one at a time, was fulfilled when Jesus gave His life for all people for all of time.

But the altar's position in the Tabernacle is interesting. In relation to the cross shape made by the furnishings, the altar would be where the base of the cross was, before getting to the body. In the Tabernacle, before accessing the person of God, the sacrifices had to be made. Before we can access the Father, we must accept Jesus' sacrifice for our sin. Our recognition of our sin and His death on our behalf is the foundation of our relationship.

Many people today want to jump straight to accepting the *love* of Jesus without talking about sin. But *Jesus' love only has meaning in light of our profound unworthiness of it.* We must acknowledge our sin, repent of it, and accept Jesus' sacrifice on our behalf. The Altar of Sacrifice could not be skipped over on the way to the presence of God in the Tabernacle. And we cannot skip this crucial step in establishing His presence in the center of our lives.

Paul said in his first letter to Timothy, "This is a trustworthy saying, and everyone should accept it: 'Christ Jesus came into the world to save sinners'—and I am the worst of them all" (1 Tim 1:15). Paul makes it clear, we must admit we are sinners. And his declaration "I am the worst of them all," ought to make us pause and reflect on our own sin. He wasn't being self-deprecating. The closer Paul got to Jesus, the more aware of his sin he became. That ought to be the same for us. Not so that we wallow in our failure, but so we can repent from them and not be entangled with sin any longer!

The altar burned up sacrifices for sin. Total and complete annihilation of the sacrifice reminds us that when we repent from our sin and accept Jesus' sacrifice for the punishment we are due, we are made completely new. Nothing is left over from our sin when we give it to Jesus. The old is completely gone, and the new is completely here.

For us to have Jesus at the center of our lives, where we know Him and are known by Him, we must continually admit our sin, repent from it, and praise Jesus for the sacrifice He made to free us from its power.

You might be thinking, "I repent of sin, but I keep doing it!" Or, "I try to give up sin, but I can't seem to kick this." Remember, the altar of sacrifice was only the starting point. Jesus' sacrifice for us, and our acceptance of it, is only the starting point of His centrality in our lives.

If the only relationship we have with God is as the Savior of our souls from the death of sin, we will be saved; but we will not experience the fullness of life with Him. The Altar was in an outer courtyard; to be close to God's heart, we must continue further in.

Laver

After the altar of sacrifice sits the bronze laver, or washbasin. Priests washed themselves in it to be purified before entering the inner parts of the sanctuary. In relation to the cross layout of the Tabernacle, the laver was at Christ's feet.

A wash basin at the feet reminds us immediately of Jesus washing His disciples' feet. He did it to set an example, "Now that I, your Lord and Teacher, have washed your feet, you also should wash one another's feet. I have set you an example that you should do as I have done for you" (John 13:14-15).

Making Jesus the center of our lives means not only keeping ourselves clean from the dirt of the world, but humbly serving others, helping them to do the same thing.

If you feel stuck at the altar, stuck in sin spirals that you can't shake, I ask how well do you serve others? How willing are you to bend down into their mess and help them wash clean? Jesus makes us clean not solely so we will be clean, but also so we can serve others. Jesus set the ultimate example of humility, and for Him to be the center of our lives, we must also pursue humility.

You might think, "I serve all the time. I always put others before me. But I am left feeling tired, and empty. I'm burned out." Remember, the laver is not the heart of the Tabernacle. It's still in the outer courtyard. If the measure of our relationship with God is how much and how well we serve, we will get burned out. We cannot have Jesus at the center of our lives without humble service to others. But humble service to others is not the core of the centrality of Christ in us.

If you're feeling burned out in ministry or life in general, I must ask, are you defining your worth by what you do? Are you worshipping by serving a God you truly know, or are you worshipping service?

Let's go inside.

After washing in the laver, the priests of the Tabernacle were allowed in the Holy Place. This was the portion of the Tabernacle was the only way to access God's throne—the Holy of Holies. And in the Holy Place, there were three more furnishings for us to explore. We'll discuss two of them and come back to the third at the end.

Table

There was a table on the north side of the Holy Place. On this table, the priests kept twelve pieces of baked bread. Twelve to represent the twelve tribes of Israel. The bread was a sacrifice given by the people, and it served as food for the priests.

The priests relied on God to provide for their needs. He consecrated the bread for the priests to eat. And He provided the manna from which the bread was made. They knew by experience that without God, they would starve.

We must understand that nothing satisfies like Jesus. Jesus told a crowd of hungry followers, "I am the bread of life. Whoever comes to me will never be hungry again" (John 6:35). He is the bread of life, and the only one who can meet all of your needs. He is the one who makes promises to you, *and* He is the one who keeps them.

Consider Psalm 37:4, "Take delight in the Lord, and he will give you the desires of your heart." I don't know about you, but I think bread is delightful. Fresh baked, warm from the oven, a little bit of butter? *Delightful.* Even more delightful is the presence of God in your life. If you want to know God and be known by Him, delight in finding your fulfillment in Him. When Jesus is the center of your life, your desires will be for Him and met by Him.

The table in the Tabernacle reminds us that to have Jesus at the center of your life, you must look to Him for your sustenance. Nothing else will satisfy. Looking to other means, be it relationships, wealth, prestige, or power, will keep you hungry and searching for more.

Looking at the layout of the cross, the Table would be where Jesus's left hand was nailed. It is widely agreed that in near east culture, the left hand was less favorable than the right hand. While both places on either side of the King are honored, the right hand had more importance. So perhaps, the provision Jesus gives to us is less important than what we do to honor Him.

Lampstand

The lampstand was on the south side of the Tabernacle. Moses was instructed to keep it lit at all times. It was one of the main jobs of the priests. Very practically, this lampstand gave light to the Tabernacle which would otherwise be completely dark due to all the thick curtains. But symbolically, it pointed straight to Jesus.

Jesus said, "I am the light of the world. If you follow me, you won't have to walk in darkness, because you will have the light that leads to life" (John 8:12). The lamp illuminated the way through the Tabernacle all the way to God the Father. Jesus illuminates the way to God, out of darkness and into glorious light.

Jesus is the light of the world, but so are you! "You are the light of the world—like a city on a hilltop that cannot be hidden. No one lights a lamp and then puts it under a basket. Instead, a lamp is placed on a stand, where it gives light to everyone in the house. In the same way, let your  good deeds shine out for all to see, so that everyone will praise your heavenly Father" (Matthew 5:14-16). The continually lit lampstand reminds us that Jesus placed His light inside you. And He did it so you would shine like Him, for His glory, so other people could see! You cannot claim to be a full hearted follower of Jesus and keep your light, which is His light, hidden.

The right hand place at a banquet was a place of honor. The right hand man is the guy who gets stuff done on behalf of the man in charge. The Lampstand was placed where Jesus's right hand would be on the cross.

As the light of the world, you are placed at the right hand of Jesus in order to get stuff done on His behalf. And He told us what to do: "go and make disciples of all nations, baptizing them in the name of the Father and of the Son and of the Holy Spirit, and teaching them to obey everything I have commanded you" (Matthew 28:19-20).

In the Tabernacle, the Holy Place could only be accessed by priests. And the lamp was only touched by priests. And guess what? "You are royal priests, a holy nation, God's very own possession. As a result, you can show others the goodness of God, for he called you out of the darkness into his wonderful light" (1 Peter 2:9).

For Jesus to be the center of your life, be grateful you have been called out of darkness; know that His light shines continually inside of you; and obey Him by teaching others to obey Him. Share His goodness, and help other people find their way into His presence. Or as Paul put it in Ephesians 5:8, "For once you were full of darkness, but now you have light from the Lord. So live as people of light!"

Ark of the Covenant

As the Tabernacle furniture was laid out in the shape of a cross, the piece at the head was the Ark of the Covenant. While the Tabernacle was God's residence among His people, the Ark was the physical seat for God's presence. The Ark was kept in the holiest place in the Tabernacle, set apart from the rest.

The Ark of the Covenant was the last furnishing in order of Tabernacle layout, but the first piece of furniture God described to Moses. In line with His priority from the beginning, this piece was all about a relationship. And it had priority status.

"When the Ark is finished, place inside it the stone tablets inscribed with the terms of the covenant, which I will give to you... I will meet with you there and talk to you... From there I will give you my commands for the people of Israel" (Ex. 25:16, 22).

In this description, we see three things:

1. The Ark was built to carry the terms of the covenant.

2. It was where God would meet personally with Moses.

3. From there He would give commands to all His people.

Inside the ark, there was space to hold the stone tablets on which Moses had written the law. God's presence would appear over this base box that held the covenant. The covenant God made with His people was His literal chair, His throne, among the people. Many times God told them, "if you obey my covenant, you will be my people and I will be your God" (Genesis 17:7, Jeremiah 7:23, Jeremiah 31:33, Exodus 19:5). The covenant, then, was the foundation of Israel's relationship with God.

When Jesus came, he said "I did not come to abolish the law of Moses or the writings of the prophets. No, I came to accomplish their purpose" (Matthew 5:17). Those stone tablets in the Ark were not void through Jesus, but fulfilled through Jesus. On the cross, Jesus carried and fulfilled the terms of the covenant between God and man. So now, *His* new covenant is the foundation of *our* relationship with God.

The atonement cover, the lid of the Ark, was where God promised to personally meet and talk with Moses. No more climbing up a mountain to have a conversation with God; God was coming down to dwell in a tent and meet personally with Moses. Throughout all of Scripture, it has been God's desire to meet and talk with His beloved creation. He walked and talked with Adam in the garden. He met and spoke with Moses from the Ark. And when Jesus came, He was known as Emmanuel, God With Us. He came to walk and talk with those He loves.

In the desert, and later in the temple, in order to meet with God, people had to go to the Ark in the Holy of Holies. And only the High Priest was allowed into that kind of intimacy. But when Jesus, Emmanuel, came to earth, God came to people. God's presence was no longer localized in the Ark. When Jesus died on the cross, the curtain that separated the Holy of Holies, the separation of God's presence from His people, was torn in two, from top to bottom. God opened the Holy of Holies up for all people to have complete access to God any time, anywhere.

Lastly, God would give commands to all the people from the Ark. The Ark was at the head of the Tabernacle, and the head gets to call the shots. Paul wrote, "Christ is also the head of the church, which is his body" (Colossians 1:18). The orientation of the Tabernacle furniture was foreshadowing Christ's position in creation. He is the head. Quite bluntly, Jesus is in charge; we are not.

Just as God gave commands to His people from the Ark, Jesus came to earth and laid down commands for us today. The only reasonable response on our part is to obey. As Jesus himself said, "If you love me, obey my commandments" (John 14:15).

Altar of Incense

Remember I said there were three pieces of furniture in the Holy Place—outside of the Holy of Holies where the Ark was. The Table, the Lampstand, and the last piece, the one we skipped before, the Altar of Incense. It sat in front of the curtain that separated the Ark from the rest of the Tabernacle. I skipped over it on purpose. But let's take a look at this final piece.

As High Priest, Aaron was instructed to burn fragrant incense on this altar every morning and every evening. The incense itself was even set apart: a very specific blend of spices which could *only* be for the incense on this altar.

The significance of incense is made clear in Scripture. Psalm 141:2 establishes the symbolism of prayers being like incense offered up; "Let my prayer be set before You as incense, the lifting up of my hands as the evening sacrifice." Even in this psalm, we see the daily rhythm of incense  and prayer reflected. 1 Thessalonians 5:17 simply says, "Never stop praying." If "never stop" feels daunting, at the very least, take on a rhythm of prayer that was set for Aaron for the incense, every morning and every evening.

When John saw a revelation of heaven, he saw elders and creatures before the throne of God and each one carried "golden bowls full of incense, which are the prayers of the saints" (Revelation 5:8). And later in Revelation, the prayers and incense are offered to the Lord: "Then another angel with a gold incense burner came and stood at the altar. And a great amount of incense was given to him to mix with the prayers of God's people as an offering on the gold altar before the throne. The smoke of the incense, mixed with the prayers of God's holy people, ascended up to God from the altar where the angel had poured them out" (Revelation 8:3-4).

This description of heaven matches how the Tabernacle was laid out—a strategic copy. In heaven, the altar for incense burns in front of the throne so its scent ascends to God. And the Altar of Incense sat directly in front of the Tabernacle throne—the Ark. And it is unmistakable what the Altar of Incense represents for a life centered on Jesus: prayer.

In order to have Jesus established at the center of our lives, we must be people who pray. The Tabernacle shows us what is really happening in heaven. When you pray, even today, right now, if you put this book down and pray, your prayers are gathered in a golden bowl and poured out into the altar of incense to be carried to the throne of God. I don't know how it all works, I just know the Bible shows us that it happens! How cool is that?

What strikes me about this altar in Exodus is what God says of it when He first tells Moses about the Tabernacle plans. "Place the incense altar just outside the inner curtain that shields the Ark of the Covenant ... *I will meet with you there*" (Ex. 30:6, emphasis added).

He meets with us in prayer.

Prayer is the very place where God meets with His people. You see, the Altar of Incense is located, in relation to the cross, at the place where the two beams intersect. Every piece of this beautifully crafted home connects through prayer. If you feel in any way disconnected from God, the Altar of Incense reminds us to pray!

If you feel far from God—pray.
If you struggle to understand or obey His commands—pray.
If you feel unsatisfied and discontent—pray.
If you feel lost in the dark—pray.
If you feel burned out in service—pray.
If you feel trapped in cycles of sin—pray.

Not only that, but this altar is located at the spot on the cross where Jesus' heart would be. Prayer is how you access Jesus' heart. And, it's how He protects *your* heart.

"Don't worry about anything; instead, *pray about everything*. Tell God what you need, and thank him for all he has done. Then you will experience God's peace, which exceeds anything we can understand. His peace will guard your hearts and minds as you live in Christ Jesus" (Philippians 4:6-7, emphasis added). God promises us that praying about everything is what unlocks the peace that guards our hearts and minds. *Your* heart is protected when you seek *His* heart in prayer.

Just like the Altar of Incense was at the center of the Tabernacle, if you want Jesus at the center of your life, prayer must be at the center of your life.

Be still and dwell

When Jesus did come as Emmanuel, God with us, He came to make a home among us in the same way Yahweh made a home among His people in the desert.

"So the Word became human and made his home among us" (John 1:14). The word translated "made his home" is literally "tabernacled." The Word tabernacled with us. Jesus tabernacled. Jesus said it this way, "All who love me will do what I say. My Father will love them, and *we will come and make our home* with each of them" (John 14:23, emphasis added).

God wanted to be present with His people, Israel, and He wants to be present with you now. "Because of Christ and our faith in him, we can now come boldly and confidently into God's presence" (Ephesians 3:12).

He wanted to make a home with Israel, and He wants a home with you now. "Then Christ will make his home in your hearts as you trust in him" (Ephesians 3:17).

He wanted to dwell with Israel and He wants to dwell in you now. "Do you not know that you are the temple of God and that the Spirit of God dwells in you?" (1 Corinthians 3:16, NKJV)

The Tabernacle was God's way to establish His presence at the center of His nation so His people would be with Him day and night. Jesus coming to earth was His way of establishing His presence with us, to make Him the center of our lives day and night. And the coming of the Holy Spirit is how Jesus' mission and presence is carried on in each believer as we become the Tabernacle for the Spirit.

Jesus wants to be at the center of your life. He doesn't want to be involved. He doesn't want to be consulted. He doesn't want your spare time. He wants to be the center of it all.

Chapter Fifteen

The Pillar

The book of Exodus concludes this way:

> Then the cloud covered the Tabernacle, and the glory of the Lord filled the Tabernacle. Moses could no longer enter the Tabernacle because the cloud had settled down over it, and the glory of the Lord filled the Tabernacle. Now whenever the cloud lifted from the Tabernacle, the people of Israel would set out on their journey, following it. But if the cloud did not rise, they remained where they were until it lifted. The cloud of the Lord hovered over the Tabernacle during the day, and at night fire glowed inside the cloud so the whole family of Israel could see it. *This continued throughout all their journeys.* (Ex. 40:34-38, emphasis added)

In Egypt, Israel was asking the questions:

Is God even real?
Is God with us here or not?
Is God good?

The decades delayed in the wilderness were a time devoted to answering those questions. The focus was getting to know God. Every obstacle and every miracle brought the nation of Israel closer to their God. As the desert sands stretched ahead of them, He unraveled the mystery of Himself before their eyes.

As a final word to those questions, God's very presence came and lived with the people in the Tabernacle.

Is God real?
I am your God and you are my people.
Is God here with us or not?
I am with you and I want to be with you.
I have sent my presence to settle in camp in such a way
that our whole family of Israel can see I am here.
Does He care?
I care by being with you and leading you. I will continue to be here
throughout all your journeys.

This final sign, the cloud of His presence, set their pace moving forward. They stopped when it settled. They moved when it lifted. God made His home among them in order to lead them.

When you become a person of stillness so you can know God, you know when His presence is staying and you know when He is moving on. You allow your pace to be set by Him. You are still, and you know

Him, so you don't push forward when He's at rest. And you don't hesitate to pack up when He's on the move. You stop and go, slow down and speed up, with Him.

We want to be people in His presence. Remaining where we are as long as He stays and going without delay when He moves.

After six years of enjoying stay-at-home-mom life, our daughter started school, and I (Kelsey) was eager to contribute to the household income.

I was anything but still. I can't say I was specifically seeking God's will for my work at that point. I would pray about it, but then go and do what I thought was best. I started the grind toward an acting career because it's what I had always wanted. In spite of my selfishness, God granted me favor with an agent in Boston. I attended dozens of auditions and casting calls. A short three months later, I got the call that I was selected for a photo shoot modeling shoes. I think I simply had the right foot size, but *why* I got the gig didn't matter—I got booked!

A few weeks after the shoot, I got a call from my agent. The client was unhappy with the photos and literally wanted me to pay them back. I couldn't have felt smaller if I were a gnat. It was the most embarrassed I've ever felt.

However, even before that phone call from my agent, I quietly quit acting. I never felt more empty than when I was at an audition or on location. I was using my skills and experience to help a company sell shoes. Cute shoes, sure, but the work didn't matter. After the shoe modeling shoot day, I stopped accepting audition notices and submitting self tapes. God used that opportunity to show me what life could be like if I went that route—the route I was forging for myself.

I would be miserable, shallow, self-conscious, constantly comparing myself, and all for what—selling products that will ultimately rot in a landfill.

Many of the projects Mike and I have begun over the years have since ended unceremoniously. Here's a list of our roles we have seen fizzle:

- Model (I told you how that turned out...)

- Board game designer and publisher

- Blogger

- Professional commercial and film actor

- Acting coach

- Church video producer

- Commercial video producer

- Creative consultant

- Voice over actor

- Executive assistant

- Motivational speaker

- Faith-based business coach

- Retreat facilitator

- Church communications director

- Church creative director

It's easy for Mike and I to look at this list and see a list of failures. We sometimes wonder if we didn't give some enough of a chance. Was it foolish or wise to move on? We often wish we were better at marketing or networking; maybe then we'd be established.

These, of course, are not Spirit-led thoughts. Looking back, we know when we prayerfully entered an opportunity, and we know when we shoved a door open. Even when we jumped the gun, by God's grace, we know we moved out when God's favor and presence did.

I believe that's the goal of all of our wanderings. Our deserts may come in the form of lackluster careers, dismal finances, loneliness, illness, longing, or questioning. But regardless of the desert, the path forward remains: follow God.

Be still with your Shepherd

True people of God stop making their own way in this world. Like following a cloud, people of God stay, and move, and exist with Him. As Acts 17:28 says, "For in him we live and move and have our being" (NIV).

This reminds us of a shepherd leading his sheep. They go where he goes. They stop to rest when he stops. They don't go anywhere without him. With him, they live, and move, and exist. God is our shepherd and He is with us by leading us.

I don't think the Bible offers any better display of the truth of "God is with us by leading us" than Psalm 23. We've copied each line of the psalm below. Notice how each line demonstrates God's desire to both be *with* you and *lead* you.

The Lord is my shepherd, I lack nothing.

With me: Shepherd is not a remote, work-from-home job. It requires hands-on work.

Lead me: The shepherd's role is to lead the sheep and provide for their needs.

He makes me lie down in green pastures…

With me: Have you tried to make a kid lie down for a nap from the other room? It doesn't work from a distance…

Lead me: The shepherd determines the pace and the place. It may require a change from your current pace and place.

he leads me beside quiet waters…

With me: Not only does God walk with you beside quiet waters, God *is* the quiet water.

Lead me: The Hebrew word for "lead" here means "to guide to a place of rest."

he refreshes my soul.

With me: Like a fulfilling conversation with a close friend

Lead me: Have you been able to truly refresh your soul without God? You need Him to take the lead on this.

He guides me along the right paths for his name's sake.

With me: Like a trail guide who knows the way because he's been here before, Jesus is with you, guiding you.

Lead me: Following God is primarily for God to increase His name and glory.

Even though I walk through the darkest valley, I will fear no evil, for you are with me;

With me: Even in the darkest, roughest terrain of life, God is with you.

Lead me: You would not willingly choose to walk through the valley of death, but following Jesus will bring you there for a time.

your rod and your staff, they comfort me.

With me: A rod and a staff are hand tools. God remains within reach.

Lead me: These tools are for correction and discipline. They aren't tools for comfort, but in the hands of a good and loving shepherd, even discipline is a comfort.

You prepare a table before me in the presence of my enemies.

With me: Sharing a meal offers quality face-to-face time. The enemies might be close, but your Shepherd is closer.

Lead me: He is the host. Where you would want to fight or flee, God chooses to stay and commune.

You anoint my head with oil; my cup overflows.

With me: In this culture, a host would keep your cup full as long as he wanted you to stay. Can you believe God keeps your cup overflowing? He never wants you to leave His presence.

Lead me: A shepherd would pour oil on a sheep to heal and protect it. A host would anoint guests to welcome and honor them.

Surely your goodness and love will follow me all the days of my life,

With me: "I am convinced that nothing can ever separate us from God's love" (Romans 8:38).

Lead me: The word "follow" here means "diligently pursue", like a commander of an army securing a victory. As we follow Him, His goodness and mercy pursue us.

and I will dwell in the house of the Lord forever.

With me: This dwelling together is the essence of what God wants most with you.

Lead me: God is leading you to a heavenly home. You are a follower until you arrive.

(Psalm 23, NIV, emphasis and commentary added)

We love being home. We are comfortable and happy in our home. When we travel, even if only for a day, we are so ready to go home to our own beds, our pet bunny, the food we like, and the sofa we picked out. We love home. No one has expectations or agendas at home. Home is where we can be still.

Learning to be still with your God is like being home. Being in His presence, knowing Him, is what your soul longs for. And every other desire in your heart is revealing a place where God wants to be.

Psalm 84 expands on the desire to dwell in the house of the Lord forever. It's not a future place, it is possible here and now.

> How lovely is your dwelling place,
> O Lord of Heaven's Armies.
> I long, yes, I faint with longing
> to enter the courts of the Lord.
> With my whole being, body and soul,
> I will shout joyfully to the living God.
> A single day in your courts
> is better than a thousand anywhere else!

> I would rather be a gatekeeper
> in the house of my God
> than live the good life in the homes of the wicked.
> (Psalm 84:1-2, 10)

This speaks of a stillness, a presence, an existence here and now. You may live in your house or your apartment, but you can dwell in the house of the Lord. You can work at your job, but dwell as a gatekeeper for God's house. His dwelling place is lovely, because He is in it.

Because of Jesus's redemptive work on the cross, His dwelling place is within you. You are lovely because He is in you. *Being still is the opportunity to know the One who lives in you.* And getting to know Him will show you that even one day with Him is better than a thousand days anywhere else. This perspective shifts our time of delay in the desert to an opportunity to dwell on the mountain of His presence. When you truly stop, and allow stillness to reveal who God is, your foundation, like a mountain, is unshakable. Nothing else in this world will come close.

BEING STILL IS THE OPPORTUNITY TO KNOW THE ONE WHO LIVES IN YOU.

I don't know about you, but there is no glowing pillar at night showing me where God is, and no cloud to show me where to head after my alarm goes off in the morning. That's how God led Israel in the wilderness. He has another plan for guiding you: the Holy Spirit. God promised this kind of direction when Isaiah wrote,

> Your own ears will hear him. Right behind you a voice
> will say, "This is the way you should go," whether to
> the right or to the left (Isaiah 30:21).

We don't have a pillar of cloud or fire to show us where to go. But we have the voice of our Shepherd right behind us with turn by turn instructions.

Jesus said, "My sheep listen to my voice; I know them, and they follow me" (John 10:27). As you get to know Him more and more, you will recognize His voice. And the more you follow it, the clearer His voice becomes.

This is how you discover God's heart through the wilderness of delay. The desert is not punishment. The desert is a divine opportunity to encounter the immovable mountain of His presence. When you embrace the stillness, you find your purpose: to know God and be known by Him. Then, slowly but surely, the wilderness doesn't feel so wild.

Our Thanks

Our Adalynne Eva, you spent a lot of time reading by yourself while we were working on these books. Not that you complained, but we want you to know that you are as much a part of every one of these stories as we are. God gave us you, and He is guiding our family. Thank you for joyfully riding along with us.

Thank you, Mom, Sally Nelson, for reading this book out loud, word for word, when I (Kelsey) couldn't sit up to edit it. Your constant and continued support have built a foundation that allows me to believe maybe I can actually write.

Becky Domeny, Mom on the other side of the equation, your passion for the Old Testament planted a seed in Michael that made this book possible. Thank you for your guidance in the Tabernacle chapters. I hope we made you proud *(If you are looking for Old Testament Bible curriculum for kids, check out her company, experiencethebiblecr eatively.com).*

Thank you to my spine team, the incomparable collective of image-bearers who got me vertical and living my life once again. Especially Kaitlyn Rumford, PT, DPT. Girl, I didn't plan on you being part of this book's story, but God placed you in it and I hope nothing more than for Him to provide you with the care and love only He can give. This book may not have been finished if it weren't for all of you caring for me when my disc ruptured. Thank you.

Pastor Rob Willis, thank you for following God and leading Journey Church to places it hadn't gone before. We went through the challenges of 2023 together and I'm grateful for all we learned from each other in the mess, the pain, and the beauty that came from it all. I'm glad we stayed.

Abi Cyr, my mentor, friend, and fellow invalid. I am grateful that God allowed us to walk parallel paths and point each other back to Him along the tear-filled journey. Thank you for helping me know who He really is.

To Michael, I know we're co-authors, but we agreed I'd do the heavy lifting on this book while you focused on the other two in this series. Your love, support, wisdom, and understanding of Scripture are on every page of this book whether you typed them or not. I'm sorry for not trusting you (and God) sooner. But thank you for choosing faith in the Lord over your wife's fear. He has given us this life and I'm so grateful to live it with you.

Works Cited

[1] All Things Considered. "Mandy Patinkin: 25 Years After 'The Princess Bride,' He's Not Tired Of That Line." WAMU, American University Radio, uploaded October 5, 2012. https://wamu.org/story/12/10/05/mandy_patinkin_25_years_after_the_princess_bride_hes_not_tired_of_that_line/

[2] Eareckson Tada, Joni (2010). A Place of Healing: Wrestling with the Mysteries of Suffering, Pain and God's Sovereignty. David C. Cook

[3] Stuckey, Allie Beth. "Taylor Swift, Submission, and God's Design for Marriage." Facebook, uploaded by Allie on Blaze TV and Blaze TV, 2 September, 2025. https://www.facebook.com/watch/?v=1459561815169600

About the Authors

Mike and Kelsey have served in creative ministry together since 2009. This has taken various forms. Mike has traveled full-time with *321 Improv* and wrote a book, *Thrown off Script* based on his ex-  perience. Kelsey has directed, written, and produced programs and videos for churches across the country. At the core of their work, their desire is to empower Christians understand the Bible and do something about it.

Together, they formed ***Outloud Bible*** (outloudbible.com), where they produce podcasts, study material, and live performances of the Bible so people can hear it, love it, and live it.

They live in New Hampshire with their daughter, Addy, and their bunny, Cinnabun.

Encourage, **entertain**, and **equip**
your audience at your next
conference, retreat, or gathering.

How can we serve you and your event?

It's our goal to give you the peace of mind that
your speakers are low-maintenance,
audience-minded, veterans of the stage,
and to help your people understand the Bible
and do something about it.

to invite Mike and Kelsey to speak
at your event, inquire at **outloudbible**.com

20-minute episodes
of engaging reading and application

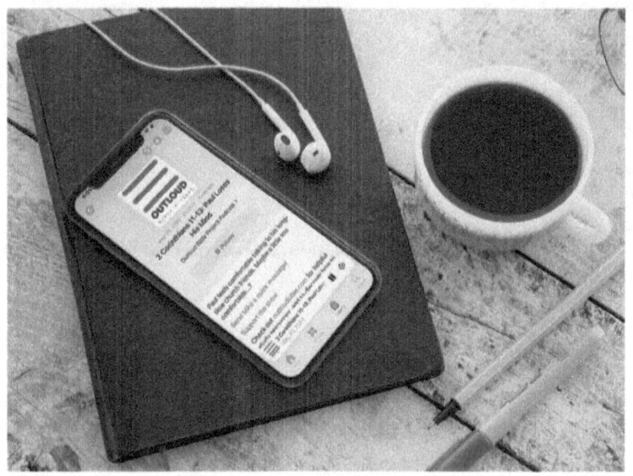

Listen wherever you listen to podcasts

learn more at **outloudbible**.com